Man as the Measure: The Crossroads

Man as the Measure: The Crossroads

Community Psychology Series
American Psychological Association, Division 27

Daniel Adelson, Issue Editor
University of California, Berkeley

Behavioral Publications, Inc.   New York

Library of Congress Catalog Card Number 77-184153
Standard Book Number 87705-058-9
Copyright © 1972 by Division 27 of the American Psychological Association

BEHAVIORAL PUBLICATIONS, INC., 2852 Broadway
Morningside Heights,
New York, New York 10025

Printed in the United States of America

Community Psychology Series

Man as the Measure: The Crossroads

Contributors

Daniel Adelson, Ph.D., *Associate Professor of Psychology in Residence, The University of California, San Francisco, California*

Morton Bard, Ph.D. *Professor of Psychology and Director, Psychological Center, Graduate Center, The City University of New York*

Daniel Freudenthal, Ed.D., *formerly Coordinator of Research and Publications, Berkeley Unified School District, Berkeley, California*

Neil V. Sullivan, Ed.D., *Commissioner of Education, The Commonwealth of Massachusetts, Boston*

Robert Schwebel, *Graduate Student, The University of California, Berkeley*

William Smith, *Graduate Student, The University of California, Berkeley*

Philip A. Cowan, Ph.D., *Associate Professor of Psychology, The University of California, Berkeley*

Carolyn Cowan, *formerly Research Assistant, The University of California, Berkeley*

Roger W. Heyns, *Professor of Psychology and Education, The University of Michigan, Ann Arbor and President Elect of the American Council on Education. Formerly Chancellor, The University of California, Berkeley*

Arthur R. Jensen, Ph.D., *Professor of Educational Psychology, The University of California, Berkeley*

Edward Sampson, Ph.D., *Professor, Clark University, Worcester, Massachusetts. Formerly, Department of Psychology, Brunel University, Uxbridge, England and Department of Psychology, University of California, Berkeley*

Preface

"Nothing," says an old Hassidic parable, "is as perfect as a broken heart." And to those with broken hearts were given the most significant tasks. There are times in human history when all the pain, the sense of injustice, the desperation of the human dilemma represented by the disparity between our ideals and our practices come more sharply to the fore. But even in such times may come an affirmation of the beauty, the glories, the aspirations of man. Such a time has been the '60s.

In such times, if you and you and you and I speak for the weight of tradition, the authority of precedent, the security of continuity and the past, youth (and the part of us that is youth) speaks for new forms and storms at the ramparts of the establishment and asserts there can and there shall be love and peace and brotherhood and joy. Youth, in a word, speaks for Man.

And youth, seizing leadership, challenges our social and economic forms, our living arrangements and our ways of dress and joining forces with the stigmatized, oppressed, and rejected—and that in us that has felt the deep hurt of stigma, oppression, and rejection—challenges our very conceptions of the nature of man.

And out of this challenge stirs and stimulates us to new ways of looking at man and his relations with his fellow man. Such a new way is community psychology. This is the crossroads.

D.A.

Toward a Conception of Community Psychology

The Implications of Cultural Pluralism*

DANIEL ADELSON

Psychology, psychiatry, the social sciences are in crisis. Alvin Gouldner's latest book carries the title, *The Coming Crisis in Western Sociology*. George Albee's 1970 presidential address to the American Psychological Association was on *Clinical Psychology, RIP*, "may it rest in peace." In Berkeley at the Free University, Claude Steiner is offering a course in Radical Psychiatry. What is the nature of this crisis? What are the implications for community psychology theory and practice?

Psychology is in crisis because society is in crisis, and society is in crisis in three principal ways. There is the crisis of man with the social structure, the crisis of man with self and fellow man, and the crisis of man with nature. We may call these briefly the crisis in democracy, the crisis of alienation, and the crisis in our ecology.

The Crisis with the Social Structure

The 1954 Supreme Court desegregation decision may be taken as a beginning milestone for the sharpening in our time of the historical human dilemma presented by the disparity between our Judeo-Christian and democratic ideals and the actuality of our practices—what Gunnar Myrdal in his classic study of Negro-white relations called the "American dilemma." At home and abroad our time has witnessed persistent demands for self-determination, for self-government, and in a deeper sense for self-identity. This is a movement that has seen some violence, but its major leader-advocates were Mahatma Gandhi and Martin

Dr. Adelson is Associate Professor of Psychology in Residence, the University of California, San Francisco.

* Based on a paper originally called "Social Crisis, Cultural Pluralism, and Social Science Theory and Practice" read at the Bay Area Psychiatric Clinic Association meeting, Sept. 23, 1970.

Luther King, who made nonviolence a powerful means consonant with the end objective—the dignity of man—a force that earned them the respect of their opponents as well as their people. This is the crisis toward the resolution of which we have seen new self-definitions by minority groups, as they have redefined their communities, their identities, and their histories. In this stride toward self-responsibility and self-esteem they have rejected the valuations of the larger majority culture and demonstrated the power, not of money or of military might, but simply of community, when this speaks for basic values. It is of interest that in this crisis there has been a turning to history as a base for self-identity—black history, Chicano history. Participants in this struggle see their roots in the past, but also look forward to the future with much more hope. They are challenging the schools, industry, neighborhoods that have previously excluded them, looking for reconstruction and change that will permit more and more to benefit and grow. It has been particularly a struggle of minorities, in which many nonminority youth and others have joined. While "cultural pluralism" has proved a great strength, it has also led to incidents of marked polarization on the right and on the left, as extremists have turned to ever more radical and militant methods for confronting each other.

The Crisis with Man and Fellow Man

Man Alone is the title of one anthology on alienation in modern society. "We live in a period," says Stein in his epilogue to *The Eclipse of Community*, "when the existentialist experience, the feeling of total shipwreck is no longer the exclusive prerogative of extraordinarily sensitive poets and philosophers. Instead, it has become the last shared experience, touching everyone in the whole society, although only a few are able to express it effectively [Stein, 1960]."

Divorce, drugs, dropping out, and delinquency mark our time. In response, we have turned to various new communal arrangements, Synanon, Esalen, encounter groups, communes, in our search for a sense of family and of community. The crisis here is between intellect and emotion; in the great need to provide again for spontaneity, for a sense of wholeness, there is an emphasis on the here and now. If in the crisis of democracy there is a turning to history of own ethnic group, of own origins, and a developing sense of past and future, the crisis of alienation appears in its emphasis on the "now" almost a desire to escape history. A long-term time perspective, as Kurt Lewin has demonstrated, is associated with high morale. The evidence of those who maintained good morale under the extreme conditions of the concentration camp also points to the importance of historical perspective.

The crisis of alienation also has its roots in a crisis of values. Gustave Gilbert, clinical psychologist at the Nuremberg trials, has pointed out that the Nazi leaders used two mechanisms in value conflict as they maintained images of themselves as righteous individuals: (a) obviation and deviation of insight, or shutting out of sight and mind the Nazi atrocities and injustices, and (b) lack of identification with the victims of injustice, or "dehumanization." Ernst Wiechert, whose door had been open to everyone, describes how to survive the concentration camp: it was necessary to become like a "stone." The question: How are we dehumanized, constricted in our emotional and cognitive horizons as we use these mechanisms in our present world (Adelson, 1962)?

The Crisis with Nature

The third major crisis, the crisis in man's relationship to nature, is interrelated with these other two. Man's increasing technological know-how has made him a master over nature, but in the process has divorced and alienated him from nature, particularly Occidental man. If the paintings of a society may be used as a projective technique to assess the state of affairs in that society, then in the Orient, man is at one with nature—a part of nature in the East, and dominating, apart from in the West. But since man is indeed another creature of nature, dependent on it, he finds that his long disregard has suddenly resulted in a situation in which his health and even his physical survival is threatened.

I shall not here try to trace out the interrelationships among these crises. I am interested that at the forefront of those struggling to solve them are minority groups on the one hand and youth on the other: minority groups who have found few roles and little status in our current structures; and youth, not yet caught up in their roles and statuses in these structures. Both are at nodal points in the crises as they are presented with the choice of fighting or not fighting in a war in which they do not believe and find unjust, and the choice of struggling or not struggling for democratic changes at home. How will they come to terms each and every one, as individuals and in common struggle with their fellows with this moment of history?

We may now ask, given these larger social crises, how has social science responded to them? And we may ask further how have individuals tried to and found ways of coping with these problems? These are not new crises, even if in the '60s they have become acute in the United States. Social science has been concerned with them for some period of time. It may even be suggested that in many ways the development of social science and some major streams and movements within social science have been responses to these crises.

We may sort out five such responses. Briefly these are the responses of (a) sociology, perhaps best represented through Durkheim and his brilliant analyses of the relation to social pathology of social integration; (b) pragmatist philosophy and psychology through William James, and especially John Dewey and George H. Mead; (c) group dynamics and experimental social psychology;

(d) what may be called an integration of historical sociology and psychoanalysis as represented by Erich Fromm; and most recently (e) existentialism through such individuals as Viktor Frankl, Rollo May, Abrahan Maslow, and Carl Rogers.

(a) It is surely no coincidence that sociology as separate from philosophy was born at the beginning of the 19th century as man, moving from country to city, became more and more aware of the significance of primary community; as growing industrialization removed him from his craft and the land and made him another robot on the assembly line; and as the growing bureaucracy made him merely a cog in the totality. Providing insights here were Tonnies with his contrast of community and mass society, Cooley with his concept of primary group, and most significantly Durkheim with his concept of anomie and its relationship to social integration.

(b) More endemically American, with its basic faith in democracy, its interest in the application of intelligence to the solution of human problems, its concern that means be consonant with ends, its core influence on educational philosophy and practice has been pragmatism. Pragmatism has had a seminal influence on individuals like Eduard Lindemann (*The Community*, 1921), philosopher of social work; Jane Addams of Hull House; Mary Follett, who gave us one of our first works on dynamic administration; and many other social-scientist practioners. Figuring among the pragmatists also is Horace Kallen, editor of James' last book and philosopher of cultural pluralism, the full significance of which has only in the past decade become apparent. If sociology has analyzed the problems of a society undergoing major change, pragmatism has been concerned with exploring and developing a philosophy for implementing change and approaches to coping with social problems.

(c) Closely tied to the pragmatist stream in ideology and in essential concern with the integration of theory and practice is the "group dynamics" movement. The democratic ethic also forms the core ideological base of group dynamics as, for example, in the classic experiments of Lewin, Lippitt, and White on authoritarian, laissez-faire, and democratic atmospheres and leadership. Even as the pragmatists were concerned with integrating theory and practice, so Lewin developed for social psychology action-research and, in Marrow's phrase, was the practical theorist, applying his insights and concepts to social problems.

Also stemming from the Lewinian tradition is the "sensitivity group" movement, which in its proliferation in schools and industry on the one hand, and in the establishment of various "growth" centers on the other, appears to have met a major need of our time. The movement can be defined in terms of an approach to building morale and productivity, a way of meeting alienation and the search for reestablishment of a sense of community, or in terms of the thrust toward self-actualization and self-realization and the recognition of the group experience (the encounter experience, the communal experience) as essential to this process.

Group dynamics also finds a significant base in laboratory-oriented experimental social psychology, which has brought insight and understanding to factors influencing intra- and intergroup relationships. It is nonetheless of interest that a key contributor to experimental social psychology, Muzafer Sherif, has been critical of its significance for social problems and has suggested that a relevant social psychology should be a psychology concerned with social movements (Sherif, 1970).

(d) With one foot on Marx and the other on Freud, and integrating a concern with philosophy and with the need to make values explicit, with history and with psychological mechanisms that are activated in large groups of people at crisis times in history, Erich Fromm has perhaps more than any other thinker raised the fundamental issues and problems of our time: the role of psychiatry with respect to the establishment; with respect to the crisis of "freedom from"; with respect to the social origins of neurosis; but he has also been concerned with suggesting answers to these problems, as in *The Sane Society.*

(e) Finally social science, here joined by great religious and social philosophers and poets—Buber, Tillich, Sartre, Camus—has responded with a movement that appears in its fundamental concerns to draw on the analyses provided by the social scientists (like Fromm's with respect to alienation and anomie), but moves ahead to provide a response in terms of the here and now. This has been the response of existential philosophy and psychology. This is the movement that comes to grips with and in direct encounter points a way to overcoming the dehumanization of man. May, Rogers, and Maslow, to mention only three, may be considered existential psychologists.

While social science has in all these ways responded to these crises, it has both in theory and in application often been caught up in views and value systems that have presented barriers to social-system change and provided a rationale and practical approach that has emphasized the need for adjustment to the status quo. Such a social science has tended to be concerned with the labeling of individuals as deviant or ill and with social-welfare and social-service approaches that have not in great measure increased the coping capacities of those being served.

It has often devolved upon the lay public to point the way to new approaches. One such "new" approach has been cultural pluralism, which carries many implications for psychological theory and practice and in particular for community-psychology theory and practice.

Some of the facets of the cultural-pluralist approach became evident from talks given by different minority-group members in two different series on cultural pluralism organized by the author (one as a course on "The Social Psychology of Cultural Pluralism," the other as a series of lectures at Temple Beth El in Berkeley).

A speaker on the American Indian, Adam Nordwall, spoke of the Indians' many contributions and then described the traditional Columbus Day celebration in Golden Gate Park as Columbus, spear in hand, and the Indian chief, tomahawk in hand, met, and both in a gesture of peace put their weapons down at the same time. During the last celebration, however, the Indian chief backed up, motioning to Columbus to put his spear down first; when Columbus did so, the chief let out a whoop, was joined by other Indian braves, who proceeded to scalp Columbus. This past year Columbus was not permitted to land at all.

Of three speakers on the Mexican-American—the Chicano culture—one young lady who was a grape pickers' strike organizer told in great detail about the grape workers' strike, the conditions in the field, a large chain store's interest in grape growing, making clear in this one example the complex interrelationships between the socioeconomic structure and human conditions.

The second speaker, a U.C. Berkeley graduate student and former teacher in the Berkeley schools, presented a rather militant ideology. What became clear as he spoke was the need to come to terms with a simple but basic problem for many minority members: "Either the system is right—and since I or we haven't made it in such large numbers we're not good, or not very good, deviant, ill, unintelligent, unmotivated; or the system is no good or in many ways no good, and we're all right." The social and clinical psychologist will recognize this as really a mental-health choice. Deutsch has pointed out how for the sake of saving self-esteem in the constructive resolution of conflict, it may be necessary to move off independently (Deutsch, 1969).

The third speaker was perhaps most pertinent of all for the psychologist and psychiatrist. A high-school girl, she pointed out that when she began speaking up in class she was referred for psychiatric counseling. Subsequently, she moved out to form a community school with friends and the help of a church.

For these four then, the cultural-pluralist approach seemed to provide (a) a base for self-identity, for self-esteem, (b) a base for challenging the system, and (c) a base for action in new directions. What is of interest is the psychological stance. With cultural pluralism comes a valuing of own cultural community both present and historical, a sense of refreshment from it, "a way of living life," a way of being that which is essentially human without rejection of the right of others to their culture, whether this be primarily associated with ethnic group, religion, nationality, place of birth, or other factors. If, as Carl Rogers has pointed out, self-acceptance and other acceptance are two parts of the same dynamic interplay, then we may suggest that the value placed on own culture and community on the one hand seems deeply tied to self-respect, and on the other to respect for others and their right to their culture.

Another aspect of cultural pluralism is often a turning back to the root or native language. Zionists, for example, rejected Yiddish, the language of the ghetto, and turned to Hebrew as the core language in their search for a positive self-identity.

As another example, in *Tepotzlan*, Redfield's study of the diffusion process of Spanish among native Indians, the illiterate Tonto, "who is usually not interested in books after brief schooling or in writing of any form, does feel a need for writing into a copybook the *corridos*, or popular songs, which express the values and ideals of the contemporary people, which sing the praises of their heroes of the revolution, like Zapata. This literature, Redfield says, does not merely persist, it thrives."

Further, Redfield notes a short-lived attempt by a group of Tepotzlan intellectuals to start a reform movement. Part of this movement was a purification of the native tongue, *nehuatl* (Redfield, 1930). These examples, of course, raise the question as to whether "civilized" ways can be diffused.

Tied to turning back to one's own language, it may be suggested, is the creation of a sense of shared destiny or of community with one's own historical group, a positive valuation of this group, which as the source of one's identity needs to be valued if one is to value self, and a rejection of the explicit or implicit negative valuations of the larger culture, a rejection of the "look me over, but don't touch" approach, which Joshua Fishman described as the implicit message of "Anglo-conformity," or the lack of reality for the vast bulk of our citizens of the "melting pot" philosophy; which Israel Zangwill and Emma Lazarus held forth as the American ideal, but which Moynihan and Glazer have pointed out simply didn't happen (Gordon, 1964; Glazer and Moynihan, 1970).

The fact is that though one may overtly deny one's own identification with a particular group, if one is objectively identified as a member of that group by others, there is strong likelihood that if one dislikes this group, one is highly self-rejecting (Adelson, 1970). Kurt Lewin spoke of this self-rejection in talking of self-hatred among Jews. In a study of attitudes toward first names, I specifically found that dislike for one's own first name if one was objectively identified (that is, called this name by others), was in almost every case associated with self-rejection. Most briefly we suggest that self-acceptance or self-esteem is developed and fostered in the family or peer group, where the individual finds basic "homonomy," or belongingness, which Andras Angyal and others see as one of the basic needs or strivings of men. Minority members, finding an anchor of strength in their smaller minority group, value their own groups and are able to reject the negative valuations of the larger culture (Adelson, 1964, 1970).

But as the individual needs his smaller group, which in the "primary" instance is the family, so the family or the individual through the family needs the larger community of shared or common destiny that may be provided through this "culture."

There is no need here to substantiate the ubiquity of the "family" as the core group for the individual. What is of interest is the finding of Cervantes and Zimmerman that the successful family is part of a group of five or six other families that share its values and norms and with which it meets regularly, for we begin to realize the significance of the social network as this eventually has impact on and is supportive of the individual (Zimmerman & Cervantes, 1960). The question: Could cultural pluralism be a significant approach to overcoming the anxiety of loss of extended familial community for our middle-class white society as well as for our so-called "minorities"?

In addition to the need for homonomy, man has one other basic need or striving, according to Angyal, and that is autonomy, the need for independence, for self-determination. This need is highly related to group belongingness, to homonomy, although at first glance they may seem sharply opposed. It is through the belongingness to the minority group that one has independence, a base for asserting oneself with respect to the wider majority, though, to be sure, there are many other factors associated with independence, as Crutchfield and others have pointed out. Thus in one's subculture, one finds identity, a common destiny and a base for self-determination.

But self-determination (autonomy) is not a static entity. The move toward independence for the individual may be seen as a process; unless the process is understood, we may react punitively at times of challenge to authority, a challenge that may represent a significant stage of the process. A punitive reaction at this stage may result in continued dependence or a hardening of lines and a complete break with authority.

The process of resolving problems both around homonomy and autonomy has been made clear through the theory of group development, which Bennis and Shepard (1960) have described and outlined in great detail. Indeed, this is a psychological theory of democracy. The theory outlines six phases in group development, three of which are concerned with resolution of the authority or power problem, and three concerned with the interpersonal or acceptance of self and others problem. These are respectively: (a) dependence (b) counterdependence, (c) resolution, (d) enchantment, (e) disenchantment, and (f) consensual validation.

In the first three phases members tend to move from dependence on the leader to counterdependence, to rejection of the leader as an authority figure as the control and power problem is resolved; in the last three phases they move from enchantment to disenchantment with each other and finally to open and direct communication as the interpersonal affection and acceptance problem is resolved.

These six phases may be compared and contrasted with the six phases or steps in ethnic assimilation conceptualized by Andrew Greeley: (a) culture shock, (b) organization and emerging self-consciousness, (c) assimilation of the elite, (d) militancy (e) self-hatred and antimilitancy, and (f) emerging adjustment (Greeley, 1969).

I quote Greeley in describing these phases more fully: In Phase 1, in ethnic assimilation, *culture shock,* "the immigrant group has just arrived in the host society. The patterns of behavior that were established in the Old World are jolted and jarred. The old culture is felt to be under savage attack and the members of the immigrant group are frightened and disorganized. The leaders, such as they are, are not sure that they can hold their people together, and the outside society keeps up a drumfire of criticism. Almost all the newcomers are poor, and they work (when they find work) at the most menial and poorly paid tasks . . . sheer survival is the only issue." [Greeley, 1969, p. 31.]

We may compare this phase with the "dependency" Phase 1 of group development, attended as it is by much anxiety and the denigration of authority.

In Phase 2 in ethnic assimilation, *organization and emerging self-consciousness*,

"the immigrant group begins to become organized; its clergy, its precinct captains, the leaders of its fraternal organizations, its journalists, become the key figures in the communities. The immigrants are learning the language and their children are becoming 'Hibernicized' in the public schools (or if one happens to be Catholic, in the Irish Catholic schools). The newcomers are clawing their way up the economic ladder and becoming semi-skilled, occasionally even skilled workers. Some of the brighter young people are embarking on professional careers. Having survived the first trauma of integration, the elite of the community now becomes concerned about whether that which is distinctively theirs is going to be lost in the assimilation process. The language, the culture, the religion of the Old World must somehow be preserved—although almost everyone agrees that the group must also become American. There is not much leisure and not much money, but enough for self-consciousness and ethnic pride to begin to assert themselves, and the political leaders of the community become skilled in bargaining for concessions in return. . . ." [Greeley, 1969, p. 32.]

While in Phase 3, *assimilation of the elite*, ambivalence begins to emerge. "The immigrant group has managed to climb at least partially into the lower middle class. Its members are storekeepers, artisans, skilled workers, clerks, policemen, firemen, transit workers, and militant trade unionists. Money is scrimped and saved to provide for the college education of promising young men and even of young women who are expected to become schoolteachers. The group's pride increases; though it is still diffident toward the world outside, there is a tinge of resentment and anger beneath the diffidence."

These three phases in ethnic assimilation may be compared with the counterdependence Phase 2 in group development: the diffidence changing to anger and resentment may be compared with the growing disenthrallment with the staff member, which in the resolution Phase 3 of group development reaches a climax in the rejection of the trainer in one role and his reacceptance in another, and is also comparable to Phase 4 in the acculturation process—*militancy.* *

Militancy:

> "In the fourth phase, the immigrant group has become fully middle class and even edges toward upper middle class. It now is thoroughly, and at times violently, militant. It has sources of power; it has built up a comprehensive middle culture; it does not need the larger society (or so it thinks), and wants as little to do with it as possible. Its members are warned of the dangers of associating with the larger society, and simultaneously are urged to become better at everything that society does." [Greeley, 1969, p. 32.]

Phase 4 of group development, *enchantment* with the members of the group, compares with Greeley's Phase 4 in terms of the development of a variety of ethnic institutions.

> "Thus, American Catholicism has generated a Catholic lawyers' guild, a Catholic physicians' guild, Catholic sociological, historical, and psychological societies, Catholic hospital wings, and indeed, Catholic versions of just about everything else to be found in the American culture." [Greeley, 1969, p. 32.]

Phase 5 of group development, *disenchantment,* seems directly comparable to Phase 5 of ethnic assimilation, *self-hatred and antimilitancy.*

> "In the fifth phase, the ethnic group is generating a substantial upper middle and professional class. Its young people are going to college in larger numbers and many are becoming successful and economically well-integrated members of the larger society. There is no question, as in the case of the earlier elites, of these new and much larger elites alienating themselves from the immigrant group; but from the perspective of full-fledged members of the larger society, they are acutely embarrassed by the militancy, the narrowness, the provincialism of their own past, and by the leaderships of organizations which seem to have a vested interest in keeping that past alive. Self-hatred, latent in the first three phases and hidden behind militancy in the fourth phase, finally comes out in the fifth phase, and devastating criticism is aimed at almost every aspect of one's own tradition and almost every institution which strives to keep one's culture alive. Yet, for most of the self-critics, there is no

---

* These phases may be compared to Sivadon's statement that chronic patients should join together to complain about administration as a phase in their recovery (Sivadon, 1959). In this way aggressions are turned outward and not repressed.

thought of abandoning the ethnic community or its culture completely. There are intense, emphatic demands for drastic and immediate modernization—demands which cannot be met—and intense ambivalence toward the ethnic group. The self-critics cannot live with their ethnic background, and they cannot live without it." [Greeley, 1969, p. 34.]

And finally, the understanding and acceptance, Phase 6 in group development, *consensual validation,* appears quite directly comparable to Phase 6 in ethnic assimilation, *emerging adjustment.*

"Another generation appears on the scene, securely upper middle class in its experience and equally secure in its ability to become part even of the upper class. Such a generation is quite conscious of its ethnic origin; it does not feel ashamed of it and has no desire to run from it, but neither is it willing to become militantly aggressive over its ethnicity. It cannot understand the militant defensiveness of the fourth phase or the militant self-hatred of the fifth, and sees no reason in theory or practice why it cannot be part of the larger society and still loyal to its own traditions. There is a strong interest in the cultural and artistic background of one's ethnic tradition. Trips are made to the old country, no longer to visit one's family and friends, but out of curiosity and sometimes amused compassion at how one's grandparents and great-grandparents lived. Many elements of the ethnic traditions survive, some on the level of high culture, some in a continuation of older role expectations. The younger members of the ethnic groups, indeed, delight over these differences that they find so "interesting" and so much fun to explain to friends and classmates of other ethnic groups.

"It is about this time that the members of an ethnic group that has reached the top begin to wonder why other groups, which have not moved as far along, are so noisy, raucous and militant." [Greeley, 1969, p. 35.]

This sixth stage from the point of view of self and other acceptance is the desired one. It fits in with Carl Rogers' hypothesis and Emmanuel Berger's finding that self-acceptance and other acceptance are two interdynamically related aspects for the individual, but that this is a process and the goal of a process over several generations.

At the Multi-Culture Institute in San Francisco, there is an operationalized program for children at the elementary-school level. This program is focused on appreciation and acceptance of both own culture and the culture of others. It will be interesting to see whether this process can be speeded up for those who already have an ethnic identity.

Remaining, of course, is the problem of those individuals who, having no sense of firm identity of their own, may find that the way to gain such a sense of identity is through militant and at times violent action. Would cultural pluralism also provide an answer for these? And if an answer, how?

Implications for Community Psychology Theory and Practice

What then are the implications for the social sciences, for psychiatry and for psychology? First, we need much more research on the significance of cultural pluralism as a positive force for self- and other acceptance, the conditions under which this is so, the nature of the process.

But cultural pluralism, in its challenge to existing structures, in the examples it has provided of new communities and new hope for minority groups already has many implications for psychology, for psychiatry, and for the social sciences. What are some of these?

1. The first implication is that we must move toward a psychology in which Man is the Measure, *Homo mensura.* Social systems have to be examined in relation to man's needs and vice versa. When the leaders of the black community in San Francisco objected to IQ tests in the schools, they were pointing at this very problem. As psychologists we have been aware that IQ tests are not culture free. All of us have become aware of the impact of teachers' expectations on student capacities, motivations, and self-expectations. We must examine carefully tests and approaches that are "system bound" and that reject individuals who given proper conditions have the potential for growth.

2. There follow the corollaries that psychology must be concerned with the whole man—thinking, valuing, aspiring and acting man, in historical and cultural perspective. A social science that shuts values out or claims that science is concerned only with truth and has no value base is really a social science committed to the status quo with the implicit value system that of the status quo. When we raise questions about the effect on "human relations," on men's relations with themselves and others of particular social, political, economic arrangements—we, recognizing the need for reconstruction, come explicitly to grips with this value question, even if we at the same time recognize the need for a strong and central anchor of stability as change is instituted.

Man as the measure underlies R. S. Lynd's *Knowledge for What* (1939) and his call for "outrageous hypotheses." The dignity of man as the central value underlies Lawrence K. Frank's *Research for What* (1964). But more, as John Dewey stated in his 1899 APA presidential address: "The essential nature of the standpoint which calls it [psychology] into existence, and of the abstraction which it performs, is to put in our possession the method by which values are introduced and effected in life" (Dewey, 1963).

Psychology must also be concerned with men in historical perspective. A relevant social psychology, Muzafer Sherif pointed out recently, is a psychology that will be concerned with social movements. He quotes in this connection McGrath's and Altman's conclusions, after an extensive review of the small-group studies: "research in the small-group field is so segmented—in the form of idiosyncratic variables, tasks, and measures peculiar to the individual investigator—that no one has a common base from which to argue (Sherif, 1970,

p. 80). Further, McGrath and Altman maintain that this state of affairs is due to the entrepreneurial ethic, which stresses "quantity at the expense of quality in research, rigor of method at the expense of creative-theoretical aspects of science, research funds at the expense of research ideas."

Octavio Romano (1969) has also pointed out the need for social science to be concerned with historical and not ahistorical man. I will suggest to you that in moving toward a concern with the whole man, a concern with values and a concern with history and culture, psychology moves toward a growth and away from a pathology orientation.

Not only the layman, but social scientists have also tended to view certain cultures through "pathological stereotypes." In a review of studies contrasting the child-rearing patterns characteristic of the very poor with those of the middle class, Chilman (1966) found the poor to be fatalistic, oriented to the present, authoritarian, of low self-esteem, and with high marital conflict, as contrasted with the middle class who were rational, future oriented, democratic, self-confident, and so forth. This is a "pathological" view of the poor, a view that if accepted by the poor, can lead to the immobilization of self-blame and anger turned inward and hopelessness about changing social conditions. This, we might suggest, is the view of traditional clinical psychology and psychiatry and the social science influenced by these, which hopes through therapy, the provision of insight, and the resolution of conflict to help individuals make it in a system that remains fairly static.

With a "growth model" we move to concern with individuals who through group and community processes join together in achieving their own objectives as they help themselves and are not the objects of help from professionals, and as they are concerned with reconstructing social systems to provide conditions more congenial for their own growth.

This I have come to conceptualize as the approach of community psychology.

In summarizing, I would like to restate the problem as it presents itself for the individual in relation to society and its subsystems and contrast the implications of what we have said with the approaches of traditional clinical psychology and psychiatry. (See Diagram 1.)

The Emphases of Community Psychology

A core problem for the individual is how he with his aspirations, goals, education, ethnic membership, social and marital statuses, and all the other characteristics that define him makes a fit with society and its subsystems, family, school, industry, laws, customs, regulations, expectations, values, and all the other characteristics that define these, so that the individual experiences a sense of ongoing satisfaction and development. Traditional clinical psychology

Traditional social psychology and social psychiatry		Community psychology
Individual	Group	Community and sub-systems

(Clinical)	Laboratory Oriented	Active
Intrapsychic	Static Relationships	Processes
Doctor-Patient	Psychiatric Theory	Systems
Passive	and Sociological	Cultures
Pathology	Methodology	Natural Groups
Treatment and		Dynamic
Rehabilitation		Action-Research
		Growth and Development
		Commitment and Identity

The interstice between individual and group is the area of concern of social psychology and social psychiatry in the traditional modes. (See M. Sherif for a critique of traditional social psychology and the need to move toward a psychology concerned with social movements.) The interstice between group and community is the area of concern of community psychology. In the traditional mode, the major emphasis is on an individual adapting to a static society; in community psychology, the major emphasis is on the individual participating in action-research processes towards the goal of the social system-growth and reconstruction as well as personal growth and development. Eight aspects of such growth and development may be suggested: (1) Accepting and valuing own group(s) immediate and historical, as a base for identity and for positive self-valuation; (2) Joining with others in commitment to common objectives; (3) Making an inquiry (research) as to the social system factors which impede growth; and (4) Taking action to change these (action-research). Psychodynamically, (5) The individual's aggressions are turned outward and not inward toward constructive uses and goals; (6) he recognizes his successes and values his own group and (7) engages in processes at various levels—individual, group, cultural, and social—as he moves (8) toward independence and interdependence, and self and other acceptance.

DIAGRAM 1. A conception of the emphases of community psychology in relation to clinical and social psychology.

and/or psychiatry have focused on helping the individual gain insight into his conflicts, experience catharsis, resolve his conflicts in relation to a fairly static and unchanging social system in what has been the doctor-patient relationship model. With community psychology comes a shift to the view that the individual or groups of individuals may participate in a process in which social systems are reexamined and in changing or reconstructing these systems toward the goal of making a better fit for them. The significance of such an approach for minority members as contrasted with white middle class we have touched on above. If we conceive the three core aspects around which these issues may be conceptualized as (*a*) *individual,* (*b*) *group,* (*c*) *community* with its subsystems, we may suggest an evolutionary process from a concern with helping individuals resolve their problems at the intrapsychic level (the concern of clinical psychology and clinical psychiatry in the traditional modes) to a concern with exploring the interrelationships of the individual to the group and/or community (the concern of traditional social psychology and social psychiatry). The latter continues to be a fairly static model of research and/or practice so that social psychology has been laboratory oriented and major social psychiatric studies of the epidemiology of mental illness, for example, have tended to apply sociological research methodology within the framework of traditional psychiatric theory. Finally there evolves a concern in the community-psychology approach with processes (e.g., group, community organization, community development, mental-health consultation and education), with cultures and with systems (e.g., family, school, industry, neighborhood), particularly as individuals, groups, and communities move toward studying and reconstructing the community's subsystems on the basis of understanding how the structure, size, context, boundaries, and other aspects of these subsystems affect individuals in them or individuals excluded or defined as deviant or ill by them.

Broadly then, the shift is to a growth and development model, away from the traditional treatment model. It is a shift from a doctor-patient relationship to a concern with social systems and the individuals in the social systems; from the community defined as a geographic territory to the community as a system of systems, or to the community as "common destiny," and to community as "process"; from the atomistic concept of individuals with focus on intrapsychic factors to social and community psychological factors, which are concerned with systems, roles, status, leadership, process, and so forth; from an emphasis on program evaluation to an emphasis on research on the relation of individuals to groups and community. From diagnosis, treatment, and rehabilitation, which we may see as secondary and tertiary prevention, to commitment and identity, which we may see as primary prevention. From a concern essentially with mind-body problems, *mens sane in corpore sano,* to a concern with a sound mind in a sound body in a sound community, *mens sane in corpore sano in civitate sano.* (Adelson, 1970).

With community psychology, we come closer to exploring and bringing into practice the position expounded by George H. Mead (1963) that self-reconstruction and social reconstruction are two aspects of the same process. This is the challenge of and to community psychology.

References

Adelson, D. Some aspects of value conflict under extreme conditions. *Psychiatry*, 1962, **25** (3).

Adelson, D. Attitudes toward first names. *The International Journal of Social Psychiatry*, Special Convention Issue, London, 1964, No. 1.

Adelson, D. and Kalis, B. L. *Community psychology and mental health—Perspectives and challenges*. San Francisco: Chandler, 1970.

Bennis, W. G. & Shepard, H. A. *A theory of group development in the planning of change: Readings in the applied behavioral sciences*. New York: Holt Rinehart & Winston, 1961.

Chilman, C. S. Social work practice with very poor families. *Division of Research, Welfare in Review*, 1966, **4** (1), U.S. Dept. of Health, Education and Welfare.

Deutsch, M. Conflicts: Productive and destructive. *Journal of Social Issues*, 1969, **I**, 7-41.

Dewey, J. Psychology and social practice. In J. Ratner (Ed.), *Philosophy, Psychology and Social Practice*. New York: Putnam, 1963.

Frank, Lawrence K. Research for what? *Journal of Social Issues*, 1957, Supp. Series No. 10.

Greeley, A. Why can't they be like us? *The American Jewish Committee*, 1969, Pamphlet Series No. 12, Institute of Human Relations Press.

Glazer, N. & Moynihan, D. P. *Beyond the melting pot: The Negroes, Puerto Ricans, Jews, Italians and Irish of New York City*. (2nd ed.) Cambridge, Mass.: M.I.T. Press, 1970.

Gordon, M. M. *Assimilation in American life: The role of race, religion, and national origin*. New York: Oxford University Press, 1964.

Lindeman, Eduard, *The Community* (1921).

Lynd, R. S. *Knowledge for What? The place of social science in American culture*. Princeton University, 1939.

Mead, G. H. *Mind, self and society from the standpoint of a social behaviorist*. Chicago: University of Chicago Press, 1963.

Redfield, R. *Tepotzlan, a Mexican village, a Study of folk life*. Chicago: University of Chicago Press, 1930.

Romano, O. I. The historical and intellectual presence of Mexican-Americans. *El Grito, A Journal of Contemporary Mexican-American Thought*, 1969, **2** (2).

Sherif, M. On the relevance of social pscyhology. *American Psychologist*, 1970, **25**, 144-156.

Sivadon, P. D. Techniques of sociotherapy. In Mabel Cohen (Ed.), *Advances in psychiatry*, New York: Norton, 1959.

Stein, Maurice Robert. *The eclypse of communities—An interpretation of American studies*. Princeton, N.J.: Princeton University Press, 1960.

Zimmerman, C. C. & Cervantes, L. F. *Successful American families*. New York: Pageant Press, 1960.

A Model for Action Research

MORTON BARD

Recently, Nevitt Sanford (1970) articulated a question that has been haunting a generation of psychologists: "Whatever Happened to Action Research?". The concept was central to the social-science vintage years of the 1940s, a period of ferment generated by Kurt Lewin's contention that research in natural settings had both practical and theoretical significance of the first magnitude (1964, p. 165). But something happened during the years since. As the methods of social-science research achieved greater scientific purity, a corresponding detachment from the world of real people occurred. And suddenly, upon being caught in the treacherous undertow of social change, the social sciences have begun to reflect on the seminal wisdom of Lewin. The role of action research during the past 25 years has been anomolous to say the least; it lead Sanford to conclude that while "action research is still very much alive [1970, p. 3]," "it never really got off the ground [1970, p. 7]."

Lewin's inchoate formulations achieve startling definition when reviewed in light of contemporary events. He focused upon the need for research for social management; indeed, his definition of action research incorporated the concept of the "change experiment," that is, "a comparative research on the conditions and effects of various forms of social action and research leading to social action [1948, pp. 202-203]."

In order to accomplish the goals of social-action research, Lewin regarded it as essential that there be an integration of the social sciences. He identified psychology, sociology, cultural anthropology, and economics as the disciplines vital to an integrative approach to social planning and action. How prophetic. And how typical of snail-paced gradualism that the recent report by a joint committee of the National Academy of Sciences and the Social Science Research Council yielded essentially the same recommendation (1969).

Dr. Bard is a Professor of Psychology, Graduate Center, The City University of New York.

The studies described herein were supported in part by the National Institute of Law Enforcement and Criminal Justice, Law Enforcement Assistance Administration, U.S. Department of Justice.

There is evidence, however, that an awareness is growing and an excitement is being regenerated regarding the potentials implicit in the conduct of action research. Highly educated and well-informed graduate students are expressing dissatisfaction with inter- and intradisciplinary rivalries. Some young professionals are discomfited by the inadequacies of the traditional means of incorporating and transmitting social-science research findings. The better informed younger generation and the demands of a rapidly changing social order are combining to force the achievement of new scientific insights through naturalistic research. And it is becoming clear that, at the same time, the university must broaden its scholarship reward structure in ways that give applied research in natural settings parity with experimental laboratory research. All of this by way of saying that the university will have to encourage methodological alternatives without fearing compromise of quality or scholarship.

The present urban crisis offers unprecedented opportunities for research in natural settings. The staggering problems of the cities cry out for problem-solving participation by the social sciences; not for "research that produces nothing but books [Lewin, 1948, p. 203]" but for research that leads "to improved forms of action, to new ways of doing things, to new social inventions [Taylor, 1970, p. 70]." Action research can serve as an effective medium for bringing the methods of social science to bear on social problems. Many students enter the social sciences in hopes of acquiring the skills with which to induce social change. In training programs in the helping professions, the motivation to contribute to human welfare is even more clear. It is in these contexts that action research may be most congenial, most effective, and most rewarding.

An Action-Research Program in
Police Family-Crisis Intervention

Planning and action

For a number of years an urban-action research model has been emerging within the context of a university professional training program. Guided by Lewin's prescription for rational social management, the program has proceeded in "a spiral of steps each of which is composed of a circle of planning, action, and fact-finding about the result of the action [1948, p. 201]." The first in the spiral of steps has been described more fully elsewhere (Bard & Berkowitz, 1967; Bard, 1969; Bard, 1970 b), but will be summarized here.

While the original objectives of the program in police family-crisis intervention seemed modest enough, planning research uncovered an incredibly complex theoretical root structure. It became clear that the ultimate design of the program would have to draw upon the knowledge in such diverse fields as clinical and organizational psychology, criminology, psychiatry, political science, social work, public administration, and community organization among others. The wisdom of the long-standing conviction that action research requires integrated social science was to become only too clear. In keeping with the mission of the university's professional training program in clinical psychology, the following objectives served as the wellspring of the design: to develop an innovative, preventive mental-health program to serve an inner-city community (Bard, 1969); to provide community consultation training for graduate students in clinical psychology (Singer & Bard, 1970); to provide a constructive organizational alternative for an agency of local government (Bard, 1970a); and to gain access to *in vivo* human behavior in order to acquire scientific insights that would otherwise be unavailable for study (Bard, in press).

Innovative preventive mental-health programs

Those concerned with mental health and illness are now generally agreed that early detection of emotional disorder and effective early intervention can forestall long-term pathology. It would also appear that the family exerts powerful influences upon the emotional development of its members. Since the traditional helping professions have yet to develop effective strategies for early identification of and intervention in family psychopathology, an atypical resource—the police—were revealed by research and planning to have unusual potentialities in preventive mental health. Available 24 hours each day, responsive when summoned to deal with injury, sickness or trouble, the police were found to be a first-line resource agency for lower-income, inner-city residents to whom immediate sources of help are not typically available. Indeed, sensitive and trained police officers serving as "case finders" would be in the position to provide skilled intervention to troubled families or make referral of them to mental health resources. Furthermore, if supported by professional consultation, trained police officers could, in the course of their normal duties, extend the impact of mental-health professionals in the community (in this instance, the university's Psychological Center).

An essential design feature, therefore, was the selection and training of a group of 18 police officers (about 8% of the complement of officers in a local police precinct) to provide family-crisis-intervention services to a community of about 85,000 largely lower-class people. The officers' training consisted of an intensive, one-month period (160 hours) of cognitive-affective experience involving relevant subject matter in the behavioral and social sciences as well as self-awareness workshops and real-life simulations. The major training effects were expected to take place over time in the course of weekly individual and group consultations provided by psychologists subsequent to the month of intensive training.

Community consultation training for clinical psychologists

There is little in the traditional training of clinical psychologists to prepare them for the complex role of mental-health consultant. Without actual experience in applying the principles of consultation, a clinical student's understanding of the process remains an abstraction at best and a fiction at worst. A vital element of the design required opportunities for providing such training while at the same time enhancing the operational effectiveness of the policemen-consultees.

The family-crisis officers came to the Psychological Center on a regularly scheduled basis each week during the entire project period of 21 months. Each officer was assigned a regular consultant (a senior graduate student). As part of the data-collection procedure, each consultation had a formal de-briefing aspect (duly recorded by the consultant) as well as a less formal exchange on the issues. In groups of six, the 18 officers also had a group consultation provided by a staff psychologist who served, in addition, as the supervisor of the individual student-consultants for each of the officers in his group. This design feature permitted unusual educational feedback for the consultants in training.

For the clinical-psychology students, the experience offered the opportunity to acquire technical skills under unusual circumstances. For many of the students, the experience was one that severely tested their most cherished stereotypes about the police. Despite the students' personal biases, weekly confrontations in the role of consultant forced them to develop technical proficiency and professional discipline. Naturally, the stereotypical thinking of the police about students and professionals was also subject to challenge and confrontation.

An operational alternative for a government organization

Preliminary planning research revealed that the police were a primary helping source to the lower classes in both urban and rural areas. Despite the fact that between 80% and 90% of police man-hours are devoted to order maintenance and service functions, it is a fact that remains unacknowledged as police organizations continue to be structured along "crime-combat" lines. Failure to recognize adequately order-maintenance roles has been costly both in community disenchantment and in the many police deaths and injuries that are derivative of inappropriate police response to such events. (For example, the ordinary family fight is responsible for a significant number of police deaths and injuries.) Indeed, analysis of available information suggested that the widening gap between the police and the communities they served was at least in part traceable to a rigid organization, structured to perform functions at odds with the expectations of the citizenry. Highly complex social needs are simplistically met within the limitations of institutional structures formed in much less complex times. It seemed clear that the mythical perpetuation of a past reality was destructive both to the police and to the community.

The program acknowledged that since all institutions resist change, it was necessary to incorporate elements that would require rational modifications of normal institutional procedures. Even more important, the suggested changes had to be designed to preserve the organization's normal manpower allocations. The essential design component can best be described as being consistent with the generalist-specialist model.

Police precincts in New York City are organized into radio-car patrol sectors with two officers on each eight-hour tour of duty responsible for general patrol within their assigned sectors. The action research plan called for the designation of one sector car within one precinct to be manned by specially trained officers and available on each tour for intervention in family disturbances anywhere in the precinct. When not engaged in family intervention, the uniformed officers in the special car were to provide regular patrol. As can be seen, manpower availability remained constant; only the manner of its utilization was changed. One of the explicit aims (useful in countering normal institutional resistance) was to improve operational efficiency, increase job satisfaction (for the generalist-specialists and generalists alike), and improve personnel safety. An action-research program involving cooperation between two such disparate groups as mental-health professionals and police officers will founder unless the advantages accruing to both are made quite explicit. In the present instance, the advantages to both police administrators and their men were balanced by the training and research opportunities to be gained by the mental-health group. Naturally, the collaboration offered the prospect for enhancing service to the community by both groups; the advantage for the community residents regularly served by both was also made explicit, and indeed could be regarded as self-evident.

Finally, the program's evaluation (in Lewinian terms: "fact-finding about the result of action") required procedural changes in the cooperating agency. In this case, family fights traditionally occupy a kind of "nonevent" status except when they result in injury, death, or court action. The design of the program required information on all such occurences to be recorded on newly devised forms and processed in new ways. In addition, similar information was collected in another precinct for comparison purposes. Such procedural changes, if rational, can serve not only to facilitate evaluation but also can themselves be adapted later for routine use by the organization. Indeed, after the present program was concluded. The data-collection procedures were incorporated for use throughout the police department, thus evidencing organizational change derivative of only one aspect of the project's original design.

A human behavioral research strategy

Action research has, perhaps most importantly, still another clear advantage. In addition to inducing social change and measuring its effects (research for social management), it also encourages the derivation of unusual observational methods and hence unusual understandings of human behavior. It is in this connection distinct from program evaluation that the project in police family-crisis intervention has much to offer by way of illustration.

The question of aggression, for example, has occupied a position of some importance in the behavioral and social sciences. Aggression and violence have been considered from many perspectives ranging from theory construction to laboratory research and animal ethology; but the spontaneous nature of human aggressive behaviors have largely defied meaningful study. In the program described here, there was an opportunity to acquire naturalistic data through the utilization of trained observers for whom the management of human aggression is a primary function. Furthermore, training police officers for social-science research roles merely involved sharpening already existing skills. After all, policemen are unusually sensitive observers of human behavior anyway, if for no other reason than that their own survival is dependent upon their ability to observe behavior with competence. It should be noted that in the police family-crisis intervention program, the observations were carried out with the knowledge, indeed at the invitation, of those being observed. The officers could, by law, enter a home only on the explicit invitation of the families visited. Finally, the usually exploitative quality of much community research was absent since the police were delivering a unique service in the course of their collection of data on the origins of family aggression and violence.

The 21-month program provided data about 962 families whose difficulties resulted in 1,375 appeals to the police for help. Surprisingly little is known about such families or about the circumstances that lead to police intervention. The absence of the most elementary descriptive information about fighting families is impressive: How frequently is actual violence or the threat of violence involved? How often does the difficulty involve marital partners or children? Is alcohol use a significant factor? What do the disputants expect of the police? How frequently are young children observers of parental violence and subsequent police intervention? The scarcity of information relating to these and other questions bears mute witness to the reluctance of social science to immerse itself in naturalistic research. It is hoped that some of the questions to be answered by the data collected in the course of this action program will add dimension to knowledge in the areas of aggression, violence, family interaction, and modern law enforcement to name but a few. One thing appears certain: the issues touched upon by the methods employed have a universality that crosscuts a number of factors—social class, ethnic, rural-urban, and economic. Continued application of the basic method (with necessary variations) in different settings will greatly enrich the knowledge yielded by this early effort.

An Action-Research Program in Police Conflict Management

"Succeeding experiments with other community subsystems might well be organized around different social tasks and group compositions. It is inherent in the experimental process to proceed from gross to finer comparisons. Each succeeding experiment thus contributes new and more refined knowledge to solution of the social problem under consideration [Fairweather, p. 210]."

Planning and action

The program in family-crisis intervention was a reconnaissance, and in Lewinian terms the first in the spiral of steps leading to rational social management. Its value as a reconnaissance, or demonstration, was established by the evaluation primarily of its crime-prevention implications (Bard, 1970 b). There was, for example, an absence of family homicides in families known to the family unit, a decrease in family assault arrests, a total absence of injuries to police officers, and a significant increase in police utilization of social and mental-health agencies.

The second in the spiral of steps ("planning, action, and fact-finding about the result of the action") should, however, seek to introduce modifications in the original plan and afford an opportunity to gain new insights regarding the action techniques employed. At the conclusion of the demonstration in family-crisis intervention, there were a number of outstanding questions that required further consideration: (a) Were the positive results derivative of the "Hawthorne effect"? (b) Was the method of training the police officers (cognitive-affective) significantly better than more traditional (cognitive) ones would have been? (c) Since the officers were selected from among volunteers, was it the training or their natural talent and motivation that contributed to the success of the program? (d) Would the methods employed be as successful with randomly selected recruits as it had been with experienced volunteers? (e) Could community response be measured precisely? (f) Could the principles of family intervention be generalized for managing conflicts that did not involve family members? (g) Could training time be reduced without sacrificing effectiveness to decrease the administrative costs and thus encourage police departments to incorporate the methods employed. The second in the spiral of steps had to be designed to address these questions.

Systematic planning research revealed an urban setting particularly congenial to the objectives of a second-stage action program. New York City has a municipal police department specifically structured to meet the security needs of public-housing developments. There are 172 such developments (largely high-rise), which house more people (660,000) than there are residing in the cities of Boston or Cincinatti. A police organization administered by the New York City Housing Authority and consisting of 1,500 personnel provides

24-hour, highly sophisticated police services to the residents of these projects, many of which are located in high-crime areas. The officers have complete parity with the New York City Police Department, wear the same uniforms (with a distinctive sleeve patch), are armed, have the same powers and receive the same salaries; their on-duty jurisdiction, however, is restricted to the housing projects to which they are assigned. It is standard procedure for the men to be assigned to specific housing developments as permanent staffs.

The action design of the current program has been described elsewhere (Bard & Zacker, 1970) but will be summarized here. The program was organized in two stages.*

Recruit training phase. Concurrent with 13 weeks of Police Academy training, an entire recruit class attended the Psychological Center of the City College, the City University of New York, one-half day each week for 12 weeks. The recruit class was randomly separated into two groups:

Conflict management group: 24 recruits and six senior patrolmen received 42 hours of affective-experiential training designed to improve their conflict management skills.

Behavioral and social science (BASS) group: 30 recruits received 42 hours of conventional, cognitive training covering a broad range of the behavioral and social sciences.

Just before graduation from the Housing Police Academy and assignment to patrol, 14 of the recruits from the conflict-management group were randomly selected and assigned to staff two preselected housing projects, with three of the conflict-management-trained senior patrolmen in each. Five of the recruits from the BASS group were randomly selected and assigned as two-thirds of the police complement of a third preselected housing project. A fourth preselected housing project served as a control, with its normal complement left unchanged.

Consultation phase. Subsequent to assignment, the police staffing the two conflict management projects took part in once-weekly discussion groups and in once-weekly individual consultations with graduate students in clinical psychology or with Fellows in Community Psychiatry from the Columbia University College of Physicians and Surgeons Division of Community and Social Psychiatry. This phase lasted three months.

Subsequent phases that followed in the current project include: (*a*) an on-call consultation phase (including continued data collection) and (*b*) a phase that resulted in the analyses of data deriving from both the current project and the previous demonstration in family crisis intervention.

* This summary is excerpted from the Final Report of the first phase (Grant, N.I. 028) of a continuing program "Police Management of Conflicts Among People" submitted August 1970 to the National Institute of Law Enforcement and Criminal Justice, U.S. Department of Justice.

Extensive procedures to evaluate the effects of conflict-resolution training undertaken during the current project include:

(*a*) Evaluation of attitudes and social awareness of recruits before and after the initial recruit-training phase.

(*b*) Evaluation of attitudes of police and consultants before and after the consultation phase.

(*c*) Evaluation of community attitudes toward the police of the four study housing projects just prior to assignment of the police to their projects and again one year later. This will measure changes in community attitudes toward those officers who received training designed to increase awareness of human behavior.

(*d*) Longitudinal evaluation of a number of police-performance criteria in each of the four study housing projects.

(*e*) Analysis of data regarding interpersonal conflicts in which conflict-resolution-trained officers intervened.

(*f*) Analysis of data regarding family crises processed by family-crisis-intervention-trained officers (during the previous demonstration project).

The present program also permitted some refinements in method to be made. New data-collection procedures, for example, were devised that were intended to reduce sources of error in data analysis. In the original program, a data form was completed by the police officers, then coded for keypunching and subsequent processing. In the present program, a comprehensive self-coding form was devised that the officers can complete themselves, thus presumably reducing coding errors.

The one-year housing-police program is nearing completion. Before long, the community-attitude survey will be readministered in the housing developments previously surveyed. Prestudy baseline data have been collected on a number of variables regarded as essential for enabling measurement of change over time in the study housing developments. The data from a variety of measures of attitudinal changes, if any, in both policemen and consultants are being analyzed as are the research data on family crises from the original program. Finally, we shall soon begin our processing and analysis of both the evaluation data and the psychosocial research data derived in the course of the housing study.

Discussion

At this point, perhaps it should be emphasized that action research as conceived here is only one avenue to social-science relevance. It appears to be a methodology that is particularly congenial to the proposition that the social scientist can bring his unique skills to bear upon social problems without sacrificing humanitarian values. It provides a medium for effecting changes in public policy within the context of a learned discipline. It helps to clarify the differences between the responsibility for working for social change through political action as a citizen and the responsibility for applying the skills and knowledge of social science to the processes of change. This is not to imply that these are mutually exclusive responsibilities. They are not. But too often the differences are unclear and have unfortunate consequences. Social scientists frequently take on roles as political essayists, as writers of social criticism, or as community leaders—activities that, while laudatory as responsible roles of informed citizens, fail to exploit the creative and unique potentials of the social-science disciplines.

Much of this confusion is the natural by-product of the basic altruism, sensitivity, and humanitarianism of those who enter the fields of social science. But frustrations with the "value-free" (or is it valueless) methodology of social science cause many of the most promising among us to sacrifice the formal disciplines for human relevance as we despair of the possibility of ever reconciling the two (Hampden-Turner, 1970).

Action research as described here does offer a methodologic alternative to, among others, the descriptive-theoretical and laboratory models. It encourages action as well as thought; it engenders a gratification that derives from involvement in social change and for which there is clear accountability in the use of a learned discipline. There are relatively few methods in which the researcher's social accountability is as clearly defined as it is in social-action research. Certainly it is an accountability of a far different order than that of the citizen who engages in political or social action in order to induce change.

The programs described above are representative of the kinds of responsibilities action research entails. The approach involved analysis of a social system (the police) and the design of systems change to improve the delivery of social and mental-health services. Statistical probabilities alone attested to the real dangers inherent in altering the system. In designing an approach to human aggression and violence, miscalculation could have had serious consequences, that is, death or injury. It is the kind of sobering responsibility and accountability that perhaps explains in some measure the compulsion to labor in safer vineyards.

As for responsibility to the community, what more potentially volatile system to work with in these times of inner-city tension than the police? In an era of simplistic polemics and ready confrontation, cooperating with "them" (the police) surely would have mobilized the more militant community monitors of establishment exploitation. That none was forthcoming in well-organized, inner-city communities signified a rational community response to relevant social science. Indeed, an attack by campus radicals, which flagrantly distorted the objectives of the first project, was quickly, quietly, and efficiently aborted by community pressure.

And at a time of increased social polarization, how much safer within the university for the researcher to avoid any involvement with the police? It is a social system almost universally reviled by academe as being beyond redemption.

But if action research is to fulfill its promise, its fields of endeavor must be those unsafe systems that offer the greatest opportunities for constructively affecting public policy and human welfare, while at the same time increasing understanding of people. To be relevant, the methods of social science must encourage and reward those who dare to expose themselves in the arenas of action.* There are many systems within society awaiting imaginative social inventions, but nearly all of them require real-world sophistication, tolerance for ambiguity, and frustration (dynamic social systems necessitate flexible action-research designs that can accommodate quickly), social accountability and responsibility, and perhaps most of all, the disciplined approach of the social scientist.

A final word to the potential action researcher. You will find yourself occupying a mid-position among your colleagues and often the target of both ends. At one extreme, those who deify the methods of the physical sciences will condemn your efforts as failing even the most fundamental tests of experimental method. At the other extreme, reliance on any of the principles of scientific method may cause your work to be regarded as a monument to inhumanity (Hampden-Turner, p. 1). There are a variety of positions in between, some of which testify to the issues that must be resolved as the social scientist involves himself in social action. Marris and Rein (1967), for example, maintain that the systematic experiment and social action cannot be carried out in the same operation because in deferring to the logic of experimental method, one must eschew concern for practical achievement (p. 207). There is, however, a growing sense of an "urgent need for society to create procedures that will bring social change in a systematic, orderly and rational manner [Fairweather, p. 4]." There are those who are convinced that a methodology can be developed through multidisciplinary efforts to build bridges between the world of research and the world of real people.

References

Bard, M. Extending psychology's impact through existing community institutions. *American Psychologist*, 1969, 610-612.

Bard, M. Family intervention police teams as a community mental health resource. *Journal of Criminal Law, Criminology and Police Science*, 1969, 60, 247-250.

Bard, M. Alternatives to traditional law enforcement. In Korten, E. F., Cook, S. W., & Lacey, J. I., (Eds.), *Psychology and the problems of society*. Washington, D.C.:

---

* An APA division requested submission of the family-crisis program for award consideration. When the awards were made, they were for traditional, experimental research. The following year, submission was again solicited, and the outcome was as before. The research awards chairman expressed his regret in a letter that concluded with the following sentence: "They again rated your research high on relevance, but showed a preference for less exciting topics with more detail in refinements."

American Psychological Association, 1970a, 128-132.

Bard, M. Training police as specialists in family crisis intervention. *National Institute of Law Enforcement and Criminal Justice.* Washington, D.C.: U.S. Government Printing Office, 1970b.

Bard, M. The study and modification of intra-familial violence. In Singer, J. L., (Ed.), *Cognitive and physiological aspects of aggression and violence.* New York: Academic Press, in press.

Bard, M. & Berkowitz, B. Training police as specialists in family crisis intervention: A community psychology action program. *Community Mental Health Journal,* 1967, **3,** 315-317.

Bard, M. & Zacker, J. Design for conflict resolution. In Cohen, D. (Ed.), *Law enforcement, science and technology.* Chicago: IIT Research Institute, in press.

Fairweather, G. W. *Methods for experimental social innovation.* New York: John Wiley & Sons, 1967.

Hampden-Turner, C. *Radical man: The process of psycho-social development.* Cambridge, Mass.: Schenckman, 1970.

Joint Committee of the National Academy of Sciences and the Social Science Research Council. *The behavioral and social sciences: Outlook and needs.* Englewood Cliffs, N.J.: Prentice-Hall, 1969.

Lewin, K. *Resolving social conflicts.* New York: Harper & Row, 1948.

Lewin, K. *Field theory in social science.* New York: Harper Torchbook, 1964.

Marris, P. & Rein, M. *Dilemmas of social reform.* New York: Atherton Press, 1967.

Sanford, N. Whatever happened to action research? *Journal of Social Issues,* 1970, **26,** 3-23.

Singer, J. L. & Bard, M. The psychological foundations of a community-oriented psychology training program. In Iscoe, I. & Spielberger, C. D. (Eds.), *Community psychology: Perspectives in training and research.* New York: Appleton-Century-Crofts, 1970.

Taylor, J. B. Introducing social innovation. *Journal of Applied Behavioral Science,* 1970, **6,** 69-77.

Focus on Community: Berkeley

Berkeley, possibly more than anywhere else in the world, was and is the scene of the crossroads. In this first issue of *Community Psychology* we focus on Berkeley and three major aspects of change in Berkeley, all of relevance to community psychology.

The article by Daniel Freudenthal describes in moving and committed detail the complex historical process of integration of the Berkeley school system. Whatever the deeper roots of process and change that mark our times, the battle for integrated schools, which began with the 1954 Supreme Court decision on desegregation, runs as a central strand throughout. This has been the core social movement.

Freudenthal's paper describes how a community is involved at various levels (school board, superintendent, parents, teachers, children and beyond), the enabling legislation and the commitment to values in moving toward change and integration of a central "growth" institution, the school. Freudenthal's article also touches on those aspects that Muzafer Sherif has suggested as central for a social movement, namely:

1. A social movement is a formative pattern of attempts toward change that develops in phases over time.

2. It is initiated through interaction among people prompted by a motivational base that is fed by persisting social problems.

3. It is carried out by those directly affected and by others who throw their lot with them.

4. It develops through declaration of gripes and the formulation and proclamation of platform or ideology, which imply organization.

5. It develops for the purpose of bringing about evolutionary or revolutionary changes, or of suppressing changes (countermovements).

6. Its efforts toward change are effected by means of appeals to the public, slogans, symbolisms, agitation, episodes of collective action, and encounters with the opposition (strikes, rallies, resistance, boycotts, demonstrations, riots, insurrection, and so forth).

As we read Freudenthal's committed account of desegregation in Berkeley these various aspects of desegregation of the school come to the fore within an "evolutionary" framework. If riots have marked the university scene, this major step in democratic process took place with sharp conflict, yes, but, as Neil Sullivan points out, without riots or insurrections. In these accounts and the lessons Sullivan draws from them there lies much hope. How, we may ask, will it be translated to the remaking of other institutions? What will be the role of the university, the role of psychology, and psychologists?

In these times of change youth have been at the forefront, and we have to ask how youth view these questions even as we ask how the psychologists who were centrally involved as educators, administrators, and scientists at the storm centers in Berkeley during these times of *sturm und drang* view them.

In the articles by Robert Schwebel and William Smith, graduate students in psychology at U. C. Berkeley, we have discussions by youth of research and services for white youth and for black youth.

We also have a series of articles by psychologists and educators who have been involved as central figures in change in Berkeley: head of the Psychology Clinic at the time of Cambodia (Philip Cowan); chancellor during the "Free Speech"' years (Roger Heyns); director of the project set up to assess desegregation in the Berkeley Schools (Arthur Jensen); and teacher-scientist and at the same time leader and sponsor of youth (Edward Sampson).

These papers make evident the variety of ways individual men view their disciplines and the relation of these views to the community problems of our time. They represent crosscurrents in psychology even as they represent the interplay of crosscurrents in the university and the Berkeley community.

Evolution of School Desegregation
in Berkeley, California

DANIEL K. FREUDENTHAL

In September 1971, the Berkeley public schools began their third year of desegregation without fuss or fanfare. Racially and socially mixed schools, classrooms and staff were established facts. The school bus was a necessary and accepted means of transporting almost half of the elementary-school student body to and from school.

Two years earlier, total desegregation had been achieved by mixing bodies, an essential step. Even as the children were being mixed, the long, arduous daily struggle toward integration began. This had to be an integration with focus on the quality of education and the quality of life within a school community deriving strength from its ethnic and social diversity.

Berkeley's Growing Commitment to School Desegregation—
The Wennerberg Years

Berkeley is a medium sized, racially diverse city of about 113,000 people. Presently it enrolls more than 15,000 students in grades kindergarten through 12.

There are 12 kindergarten-primary schools (grades k to 3), four intermediate schools (grades 4 to 6), two junior-high schools (grades 7 and 8), a ninth-grade campus and a main campus of a comprehensive four year high school and a small continuation school. In addition, about 1,000 preschool children receive early childhood instruction, and an adult school serves 4,000 adults. Of the school population, 45.7% is white, 3.4% is Chicano (Latin, Spanish surname); 44.7% black; 8.6% all other, mostly Asian. American Indians represent only .1% of the school population.

This was not always so. In 1939, there were fewer than 500 black children in the Berkeley schools, about 4% of total enrollment. By the mid-'60s, there were almost 6,000 or about 40%. This, as in many Northern cities, was a major population shift. The almost homogeneous white community of 1939 had

---

Dr. Freudenthal, presently a teacher in the Berkeley Unified School District, was for eight years Coordinator of Research and Publications.

become by 1964 one of the most racially diverse small cities in the nation. Berkeley was and remains a city of light industry and service trades. It has been and is a bedroom city for San Francisco. Location and climate have made it a continuing haven for retired people. It has one of the lowest ratios of school-age population to total population in California. It is the site of one of the nation's greatest universities, with the student population making up almost 25% of total population. The University of California is the city's largest employer, pouring its large payrolls and consumer demand into the city's economy. Its extensive properties provide no tax support for the public schools. As an institution and a community, it demands the most expensive education.

Berkeley's population is well educated and high in income by average standards. Its limited industry provides a progressively inadequate local tax base as public needs increase. It has traditionally had, and still has a hard-core "no" vote on all issues of public improvement, especially those related to the schools. Stand-pat organizations, continuing and ad hoc, often with overlapping membership, serve as watchdogs of the public morality and public purse. They oppose such changes in the status quo as fluoridation, fair employment, fair housing, school-bond and tax proposals, new reading methods, and desegregation.

Until about 1960, the schools, the community, and the university went their separate ways, mutually indifferent to changing times and changing needs. They refused to recognize that Berkeley was no longer lily white. Though Berkeley remained a relatively privileged community in education and income, the white advantages and black disadvantages at every point of community life paralleled those found in most Northern cities. The gaps were the same. There was more poverty than met the eye. The quiet, complacent, in-grown conservative college-business town was gone in fact, if not in "old Berkeley" mythology. It had been replaced by a rich racial mix. Berkeley leadership was at a crossroads that it scarcely recognized. Though challenged even within the white community, the still dominant conservative leadership in city and schools, often described as the "downtown boys," was unready to face that reality.

NAACP and Staats Study—The First Breakthrough Based on a Study

In 1958, four years after the Brown decision, the Berkeley Board of Education, on the superintendent's recommendation, recognized that there might be "certain racial problems" in the Berkeley public schools worthy of study.[2] Six months later a representative citizens' advisory committee was appointed and the beginning of the end of racial segregation in the city's schools was set in motion. On Oct. 19, 1959, 17 months later, the advisory committee submitted its report entitled *Interracial Problems and Their Effect on Education in the Public Schools of Berkeley, California*. The board accepted most major recommendations of that committee.[3]

Though the committee noted the fact of segregation in all schools but the high school, the issue of desegregation was not broached directly, for this was before the term "de facto segregation" had been coined. Issues of black underachievement and latent prejudice in a potentially enlightened community were emphasized. Discrimination and segregation within Berkeley's single high school were of particular concern. All of the ingredients of later minority demands and efforts were there in preliminary form. Acceptance of the report was a first breakthrough.

Overcoming resistance to change. Changing laws and changing community conditions brought pressures for change. There was the fact of a black minority population enlarged by massive wartime immigration of new members from the South, often poor, its needs neglected in community and school; its presence unwanted. There was the reality of growing white revolt against do-nothing, low-tax school and city leadership, spearheaded by more liberal Democrats. In 1956, there had been a successful struggle by Berkeley teachers against the school board and superintendent in alliance with supporting citizens to bring the teachers' low salaries up to a competitive position in the state and the area. Out of that struggle emerged an interracial Committee on the Berkeley Schools. The committee, in alliance with the local chapter of the National Association for the Advancement of Colored People (NAACP), joined forces with the teachers to elect Dr. Paul Sanazaro to the school board, breaking the conservative monopoly on that body.[4] So the stage was set for Dr. Roy Nichols, spokesman for the NAACP, to confront the board of education with the facts of interracial life in the nation and in Berkeley. He worked six months on preliminary discussion with a handpicked group of school administrators before convincing the threatened leadership that the issues of race in Berkeley education were sufficiently important and urgent for serious study.

The significance of values and commitment combined with a competent Information supply

It was only when the superintendency changed five months after the study began that the committee, encouraged by the new politically liberal educational leader, C. H. Wennerberg, got down to work. The committee, its chairman (Judge Redmond Staats, Jr.), especially its vice chairman (the Rev. Roy Nichols), with the unflagging support of Dr. Sanazaro, no longer the single sympathetic board member, and his colleague Spurgeon Avakian overcame resistance to all but one of the recommendations (see below) of the committee.[5]

The new superintendent played a decisive, facilitating role based on philosophical and political values that he considered important dimensions of the competence and commitment he had brought to his job. The board accepted his persistent recommendations.

Core of staff support in the midst of division. There were staff members, a very few, who from the beginning sided with those individuals and groups in Berkeley who insisted that the community and its schools come to grips with issues of race in the classroom. Others sided with those who opposed this modern human stance. Most were uncommitted, and though generally hostile to change would drift whichever way the winds might take them. The few who rallied to the new leadership brought with them a conviction to the civil rights cause, however arrived at.

They were a few who also brought a professional competence and commitment in their fields, whereby the superintendent, the board, the citizens in committee and as individuals should have a continuing supply of information and advice critical to decision making and within time deadlines. They brought an ability to build a position, state it, and defend it. The new superintendent recognized this and used the efforts of the mavericks, organizing them into a team of what later might have been termed "change agents." Here was the beginning of a theme that recurred time and time again during more than a decade of struggle toward desegregation and now toward integration—but hardly to perfection. A heritage of racism had crippled our abilities to deal with problems of race. So, too, traditional school organization and management tailored to a small amateur operation had made it doubly difficult to solve the substantive problems of both community and classroom.

Breakthrough. It was more than two years from that evening in January 1958, when the Rev. Roy Nichols, representing the NAACP, first confronted the board of education until the evening in spring 1960 when that board, strengthened by the presence of two progressive members, officially adopted the substance and spirit of the Staats report.

CORE Demands, Hadsell Study, and Secondary-School Desegregation

On May 1, 1962, eight years after Brown versus the U.S., the Congress of Racial Equality made its *Presentation to the Berkeley Board of Education on De Facto Segregated Schools.* First, it approached Superintendent Wennerberg with its concerns and demands. The superintendent was disconcerted by the use of the term "de facto segregation" in description of the Berkeley school system. He listened and urged CORE to take its cause to the board of education in public meeting. CORE presented its brief report before a standing-room crowd. It congratulated the board on its "giant accomplishments," but pointed out the existence of identifiable de facto segregated schools. Offering no pat solutions, it demanded that the board officially recognize the fact of segregation in the school system, appoint a broadly representative interracial citizens' committee to verify that fact, and make recommendations to eliminate or ameliorate it.

The board, somewhat shocked at its harsh impact, received the CORE plan politely if not cordially and turned it over to the superintendent for study, and recommendation in early fall, about three months later. This in itself was a far cry from the downright hostile board reaction to the NAACP proposal four years previously.

Changing attitudes. The atmosphere had changed in school and community. In 1962, four of the five board members were considered "liberal." Where individual members might go in support of CORE's proposal or as advocates of school desegregation would depend on the force of the superintendent's recommendation, their assessments of the political price, their commitment to the issues, their consciences, feelings, fears, and hopes.

The board had just become whole again. For 18 months out of the previous several years, it had been split two and two. The fifth member had resigned. The remaining four were at loggerheads over all major issues, especially those involving civil rights and academic freedom. They could not agree on anyone to fill a vacancy until election time, as required by charter.

Even so, the district had made some progress. A small tax increase was approved by the voters a few months after a measure more adequately tailored to need had been overwhelmingly defeated. A school-bond issue, half of the original proposal, was to pass in the summer of 1962, just after CORE came on the scene. That victory was accomplished on the heels of four previous defeats in less than two years. Intergroup education was active within staff and in the community. Progress had been made in interracial hiring. Services had been improved on the strength of the tax increase. An independent school-resource volunteer group was helping teachers and students on request, especially in schools in the black community.[7] For every Citizens United member to oppose tax and bond issues, desegregation proposals, sex education, "radical teachers and teaching," experimentation in general and particular, there was a School Resources Volunteer and an expanded, available—though informally organized— committee on the Berkeley schools under one name or another.

Superintendent moves around roadblocks

The superintendent had opened many doors as a proponent of both the democratic society and the democratic classroom. He had encouraged experiment. He had reorganized his staff, replacing those of the "old guard" when he could. Too many at every level were so strongly rooted in the conservative politics of the community that they were beyond reach.

To get around the roadblocks, two new administrative-assistant positions were established. One was in management generally, which eventually developed into the key position of "special assistant," "right arm," or personal aide to the superintendent. The other served a more purely staff service function of research and information gathering, counseling, advising, the superintendent primarily, but also staff and public as time would permit. The one "spoke" for the superintendent, serving as his alter ego. The other, by the nature of the job, his temperament, his social and political values perhaps more than his educational values, tended to speak out on the issues, especially those of civil rights, civil liberties, academic freedom, educational experiment, community relations, and administrative reform.

Developing an appropriate answer to CORE demands. It was in this uneven, emerging atmosphere, more receptive to change than in 1958, that the administrative assistant for research, defining his role in aggressive terms, volunteered to study the CORE report and recommend a course of action to the superintendent. The study and recommendations would be closely "supervised" by the superintendent's administrative advisory council, representative of central and field administration, his "cabinet." The undertaking was carried out over the summer. Neither public nor staff was readily available. Expert consultation was afforded by the California State Department of Education in the person of Wilson Riles, the first high official from the black minority in that department, presently California State Superintendent of Public Instruction. Continuing consultation was held with the superintendent's administrative advisory council, whose membership had negligible comment until it examined the final draft just two days before the superintendent's recommendations were to go to the board of education. The administrative assistant's task had been ostensibly completed. At that point, objections to substance and form were myriad. It seemed that the superintendent was stuck with a report that his chief advisers were trying to cripple at the last possible moment, without quite repudiating it. At the close of the meeting, the author immediately sought out the superintendent and proposed to reconcile the differences and redraft the document overnight. The report was redone and submitted to the board of education on time, its basic thrust preserved.

Board adopts superintendent's strong recommendation. Hundreds of citizens sympathetic to CORE's proposal attended the board meeting of Sept. 19, 1962 in force. CORE was prepared to hold a sit-in if necessary and to go to court to force board action. There was no need for that. The board accepted the superintendent's strong, documented recommendation to appoint a broadly representative citizens' committee to define and study de facto segregation in the Berkeley public schools and to recommend ways in which it might be ameliorated or eliminated. It refused only to approve the recommendation that committee members be selected by representative community organizations. It would seek organizational nomination of prospective membership, keeping for itself the power of selection. To this day Berkeley boards hold to that position.[8]

When the committee convened to look in depth at the facts of segregation, detailed spot maps of estimated student racial enrollment by block and school-attendance area were available. These became crucial to many committee deliberations and decisions. The staff responsible had moved quickly, with initiative.

Hadsell Committee Recommendations: The De Facto Segregation Study Committee

This committee labored for more than a year under the chairmanship of the Rev. John S. Hadsell, Presbyterian Campus Minister. It offered its report and recommendations to the board of education in November 1963.[8] Just before the committee reported, Superintendent Wennerberg, the educational leader who had opened so many doors to change in the Berkeley school community, resigned as of June 30, 1964 to continue advanced committee graduate study.[9] This freed him, in the last nine months of his administration, to push through Berkeley's first significant move toward desegregation without worrying on whose political toes he might step.

The Hadsell Committee[10] reiterated the Staats recommendations of 1958, calling for an intensified effort to get and keep a superior, racially balanced staff and thereby to upgrade teaching, counseling, guidance, remedial services, and administration. It pressed for summer-school expansion on a racially desegregated basis to meet both the enrichment and remedial needs of any who wanted these extra opportunities. It sought a comprehensive compensatory-education program from prekindergarten through the adult years, involving each school and every community resource. It proposed renewed emphasis on intergroup education for the entire staff. It suggested a community-wide human-relations commission to coordinate efforts in the interrelated areas of education, employment, housing, social welfare, and recreation.

The committee attacked the rigid tracking system in the secondary school as a cause of resegregation in desegregated schools. It recommended a four-band ability-grouping system in junior high schools to ease the rigidity and facilitate the transition between groups. It asked that original 7th-grade placement of students be made on the recommendation of 6th-grade teachers. This was indeed a compromise, because a sizable minority held that tracking in secondary schools should be abolished.

The committee came squarely to grips with school desegregation, proposing redistricting of both elementary and junior high schools, supplemented by voluntary and limited open enrollment. This first Berkeley proposal in the interest of school desegregation represented the bare minimum on which the committee could agree. For the first time, school desegregation and compensatory education were treated as inseparable ingredients of the ultimate racial integration essential to real improvement in the educational opportunities for all the children.

Public hearings. This first public meeting on the Hadsell report, attended by 1,200 citizens, was an angry and divided one. The articulate opposition was out in force. The questions raised were rhetorical and too often racially insulting. There was general white acceptance of compensatory education as long as it remained separate and apart from school desegregation. Reminiscent of the earlier days in 1958 and of the almost successful 1962 campaign for a local fair-housing ordinance, the divided community articulated its differences with a clear and ominous mutual hostility.[11] The need for a second public hearing was obvious. That hearing was held on Jan. 22, 1964 before 2,500 people. Supporters of desegregation came out in force and spoke for organizations and individuals. In the minority was the perennial tax-protest group, Citizens United, and its embryonic offspring, Parents Association for Neighborhood Schools.[12]

Emergence of Ramsey Plan—A Variation of Princeton Plan

The committee's specific desegregation plan satisfied no one. It provided for massive redistricting and large-scale administrative machinery without significant effect on racial imbalance. Its recommendation, however, specifically stated that the suggested plan was merely one compromise proposal, and it urged other individuals and groups to come up with a better one. This happened between the first and second public hearing on the Hadsell report. A Berkeley junior high school English teacher, Miss Marjorie Ramsey, in collaboration with interested citizens and colleagues, authored what has ever since been known as the Ramsey Plan. *Inspired by the Princeton Plan, the classic school pairing model, Berkeley's three junior high schools would be desegregated by requiring all children in grades 7 and 8 to attend two junior high schools. All children in grade 9 would attend what had been the third junior high school. That school would become an integral administrative part of the senior high school. The senior high school would thus be transformed into a four-year high school located on two separated campuses. As a result, all Berkeley's secondary schools would become desegregated.*

Staff Committee of Five, genesis and membership. At the superintendent's strong suggestion, the board turned the Hadsell Committee report including the Ramsey alternative to him for general staff study and reaction, with a report and recommendations due in two months.

Superintendent Wennerberg called for volunteers, five of whom would be chosen to assess staff reaction to citizen-committee recommendations. Many rushed to volunteer for various reasons. Some were eager to participate in moving toward desegregation in the Berkeley schools. Others hoped to stem the tide. Each had his ax to grind. The interracial Committee of Five, chosen in short order, selected their own chairman, an able and quiet man, more moderator and peacemaker than proponent. An elementary and a secondary principal, the coordinator of data processing who had served as staff liaison with the Hadsell Committee, the coordinator of counselors, and the administrative assistant for research made up the committee.

Whatever their philosophical, political, temperamental differences, each member had volunteered for a difficult assignment. Each had put his or her professional future on the line. Each had a vested interest in the success of the enterprise. All were fearful, reflecting the deep hostilities of a divided, if often polite, community and of a staff mirroring the divisions of community, hardly ready to accept change with equanimity. They would swim not sink together. They were flattered by the trust the superintendent had placed in them. They felt their power. Each in his own way wanted to have significant impact on the course of events in the Berkeley school community. They would use their power responsibly in a cause that would ultimately provide Berkeley's children, all of them, with vast educational and social benefits.

Staff Committee of Five, role and recommendations. Reactions were obtained on each Hadsell Committee recommendation and on the Ramsey Plan, school by school, office by office. An uneven staff consensus was obtained and submitted to the superintendent. He reported it to the board together with the committee's recommendation on March 3, 1964, six weeks after the committee had been appointed.

The Committee of Five urged the board to adopt the Hadsell report in principle. It pressed for the appointment of a staff task force, broadly representative of the races, sexes, schools, levels, departments, disciplines, opinions. The task would be to undertake an immediate implementation study of the educational and financial feasibility of the Ramsey junior high school reorganization plan, all other committee proposals, and additional staff alternative recommendations and priorities. Critical to the process would be continuing, comprehensive staff involvement. The implementation study together with the superintendent's recommendations would be presented to the board of education at its regular meeting of May 19, 1964, two months hence.[13]

The Committee of Five approached the superintendent and convinced him that it should become the steering committee responsible for coordinating the entire task force implementation study, and that the force should be divided into seven task groups, each to specialize in a major area of Hadsell Committee recommendation.[14]

The committee further recommended that it should choose a task force of about 40 members subject to the superintendent's approval. Nominations would be made by schools, departments, offices, individuals, including the members of the committee itself. It also recommended that task-force members be paid for the extra hours entailed in their special assignment. The superintendent approved the Committee of Five's recommendation in full, leaving that emerging steering committee free to do what it had contracted for.

Task-force selection, action, board decision, community division. Members of the task force were chosen for their representativeness—professionally, racially, politically. Teachers were well represented. A spectrum of opinion was essential in order that the task force could develop consensus from great divergence if not from a generally expressed desire to "do right" by the children.

Out of confrontation and encounter on the issues came what the superintendent accepted as his recommendations to the board of education.

On May 19, 1964,[15] before several thousand Berkeley citizens, Superintendent Wennerberg presented the task-force report, recommending the adoption of all Hadsell Committee proposals except those for school redistricting. As an alternative, he recommended an elementary-school desegregation plan wherein the large, predominantly black elementary schools would henceforth house grades 4 to 6, while the smaller, predominantly white elementary schools would house grades kindergarten to 3. This was another application of the Princeton model. He recommended a two-step junior high school reorganization plan, the first step effective in the fall of 1964. The single desegregated junior high school would remain intact. Children in grades 7 and 8 in the rest of Berkeley would attend what had been the predominantly white junior high school. Students in grade 9 would attend the formerly predominantly black junior high school, which would become a branch campus of the main high school. He recommended the adoption of a flexible four-track ability-grouping system in all junior high schools and the earmarking of $200,000 in the 1964-65 budget as a compensatory education fund to be specifically allocated as comprehensive plans were developed.

The board unanimously approved all but one of the superintendent's recommendations. The vote was 4 to 0, since the sole conservative member had resigned before the moment of decision for ostensible business reasons. The board indefinitely tabled the elementary-school redistricting proposal on the grounds of its political unfeasibility. The community in the mature judgment of the members was just not ready. Further, the then incumbent board pledged itself not to revive the elementary-desegregation proposal. It was bending every effort to avoid a recall election that was impossible to avoid. With a far-out plan to table, the majority of white community accepted a lesser evil. Yet, had it not tabled the elementary-school plan, recall would have succeeded.

Already the sides had gathered. At the meeting, public discussion was angry and occasionally vituperous. Immediately, representatives of the emerging Parents for Neighborhood Schools (PANS) threatened recall. The developing interracial counterorganization, Friends of Better Schools (The Friends), an ad hoc throwback to the Berkeley School Committee of 1956, accepted the challenge, vowing to support the whole program to upgrade the schools and desegregate them.

Informational Vacuum: The Significance of Keeping the Public Informed

Interestingly, no board member had seen the staff report before the meeting, nor had it been distributed to the public. It had been given to the task force of 40 members. Somehow the Berkeley *Gazette*, obtained a copy and spread the report's recommendations over the Gazette's front page. The decision to withhold the report from board and public till meeting was made by the task force steering committee by a vote of 4 to 1. *The minority of one felt that there was need for board to know ahead of time and equal need for the community to know.* There could be no secrets. Friends would be confused, and enemies would gain. Indeed, there was confusion and rightful anger in the ranks of actual and potential allies. But the rightness of the cause overcame the mistaken timid strategy. Perhaps a lesson was learned.

Recall campaign and recall defeat. Within three weeks, Superintendent Wennerberg's term was over, his professional mission in Berkeley completed. Within six weeks, Dr. Neil V. Sullivan took office, fresh from his leadership in bringing free public education back to 1,600 black students in Prince Edward County, Va. Recall, spearheaded by the Berkeley *Gazette* and supported by the mayor, was in full swing. A PANS attempt to qualify for an election during the summer when many supporters would be away was blocked by legal maneuvering. The new superintendent vowed he would leave the district should recall succeed. Meanwhile, only two board members remained to face recall, Mrs. Carol Sibley, now board president and strongly in support of desegregation, and Dr. Sherman Maisel, University of California professor. The conservative member who resigned early was gone, of course. The Rev. Roy Nichols resigned, having been called to a new pulpit in New York City. Spurgeon Avakian resigned, pending his appointment to the Superior Court Bench in Alameda County. Their replacements, proponents of desegregation, carefully selected by the board of education from among many nominations by organizations and individuals, would face regular election in the spring.[16]

PANS ran its own candidates against the remaining incumbents. The one was its president, a lawyer, advocate of the "neighborhood school," and opponent of "social experimentation with our children." The other was a recently retired school employee of 40 years, longtime principal and champion of the predominantly white junior high school, proponent of the discarded ability-grouping and tracking system.

The recall campaign was intensive, door-to-door on each side. There were those who would stand as pat as possible and who really saw nothing wrong with separate education even if it were unequal, who wanted the schools to mind their own "3-R" business. They really feared mixing with a race or races that at best were different and disadvantaged and at worst inferior. There were those who might go either way. There were those who were convinced that if public education had a future, it had to be interracial as a matter of morality, legality, and pure practical survival in an interracial community.

Superintendent Sullivan entered Berkeley to the cheers of the Friends and the dismay of the PANS. He spoke immediately to the issue of a quality education in Berkeley "worthy of imitation." He maintained that quality education fitted for this century could not be attained in segregated schools, either black or white, brown, red, or yellow. To him, the desegregation of the secondary schools was a significant forward step. But without a continuing improvement in their quality, the change could prove abortive.

Secondary schools desegregate. As the community suffered the recall campaign, the secondary schools were desegregated, reorganized, and proceeding with the day-to-day business of education. The new Ninth Grade School, formerly mostly black, renamed and with a "new image," seemed to flourish. Parents, students, teachers had been prepared and were hopeful of success. Perhaps a Hawthorne effect had set in. The formerly predominantly white junior high school, overcrowded, less prepared because it had been a privileged and a "superior" school, struggled desperately through the beginning days of change; students, parents, staff unready, perhaps a Hawthorne effect in reverse. But the school survived.

It was significant that in the preparation for changeover, the task force and central administration put almost singleminded emphasis on preparing the staff, students, and parents of the Ninth Grade School, the former "ghetto school," for their new experience, expecting the "worst."

Almost no attention was given the formerly white prestige school. Only passing attention was given the possibility that the reputation was illusory, and that among parents and staff was strong, hard-core opposition to any change in that school's racial composition or the direction of its program.

The Sullivan Years
and Their Culmination in Total Desegregation

The new superintendent did not have to leave Berkeley almost immediately after his arrival; for on Oct. 6, 1964 recall was rejected by a 57% majority.[18] The victory was tied down the following spring when the three new appointees to the board won at the polls by better than a 60% majority over a PANS slate. This was the culmination of six years of encounter in the Berkeley community and within the school staff. The new superintendent could consolidate the gains of partial desegregation and move it forward at the ripe time, just as the former superintendent had opened the door to change.

The task

It was to be four long years before the process of desegregation was completed, and Dr. Sullivan's commitment to himself, the board of education, and the minorities of Berkeley fulfilled. The time was not ripe to move head on to mix elementary schools and classrooms. There was the urgent, immediate, and continuing problem of making secondary-school desegregation work to the benefit of the students and the community, developing programs relevant to the mixed schools. The realities of increasing alienation among the students had to be dealt with. A qualified interracial staff committed to relate to, cope with, and educate the students in today's classrooms for today's world and tomorrow's was desperately needed. A never-ending professional and multifaceted communications and participation network was required literally to bring the schools into the community and the community into the schools. The neglect gap among minority students had to be bridged by compensatory and remedial programs at all grades, using the talents of paraprofessionals from within the communities of the poor and the minorities, facilitating widespread experimentation to loosen up lockstep curriculum and tired teaching, but never forsaking the less immediate goal of total desegregation. At the same time, the new superintendent had to be deeply concerned with administrative organization, structure, communications, and behavior more tailored to the calm days of yesteryear than able to navigate today's rough waters. His attention would have to be drawn to plant and equipment as it became increasingly outdated in a rapidly automating society. Above all, financing the basic and expanding needs students and community, setting the priorities and balancing them equitably would be a persisting nightmare.

The staff

The new educational leader, of necessity a political leader, brought with him minimal new staff resources: several teachers and a black elementary-school principal, tried by fire in the Free Schools of Prince Edward County; another elementary school principal, a nationally recognized pioneer in reading methods and in team teaching from a Chicago ghetto school; and a director of secondary education, long experienced in the solid academic classrooms of Eastern preparatory schools. But the superintendent had the services of a new and youthful interracial staff, many of them tested in the struggle for secondary-school desegregation. This was particularly true of the new director of elementary education and the new special assistant. Moreover, interracial representation in the teaching, specialist, and administrative staffs was steadily if slowly increasing.[19] There had been a turnover in about one-third of the district's principals. It could have been that the premium in personnel selection was no longer being entirely put on the good soldier, conforming, well turned out and "antiseptically neutral" in values and attitudes. Increasingly, the district sought lively, ardent protagonists of a human and humane classroom and community, who at the same time were competent professionals and technicians.

Soon, Superintendent Sullivan established a comprehensive public-information policy, using the many tools at district disposal. In Berkeley school circles, if less so than in others, there was continuing resistance to the release of any premature information on programs and plans. Publicity was highly desirable; it served as a chronicle of accomplishment. Those who resisted publicity seemed to favor keeping the community in the dark as long as possible and avoiding the hassle of controversy. As some Berkeley educators learned from sad experience, where an official or an agency was suspected or guilty of withholding essential information from its public, the resulting credibility gap created immeasurable damage. There would be no alternative to a forthright flow of truthful information to and from the community. There was hope in 1964 that the sound policy enunciated by the superintendent could ultimately become the general practice. There is still hope today.

New directions

The watchword was "new directions toward schools worthy of imitation."[20] The long-run direction would be toward "positive integration among the races." More immediately, special attention would be given to children with reading difficulties to the exclusion of other subjects, if necessary, until they came up to grade level. *The district would move toward ungraded elementary and secondary schools, team planning and team teaching with realistic speed, encouraging principals and teachers to develop models worth emulating. The special services of guidance, psychology, and health would be brought into the school and the classroom. Compensatory education would be made available from kindergarten through adulthood. Early-childhood education would be expanded and ultimately made part and parcel of the regular public-school program. Education in all grades would revolve around concept development through problem solving with the required skills and drill introduced as needed. Foreign language would be introduced during the early elementary years, taught daily by specialists and calculated to make the student bilingual at high-school graduation. Extensive enrichment would be the rule, featuring the field trip, the opening up of school laboratories after hours and on Saturdays.*

This new approach would guarantee the freedom of a teaching-learning process unafraid of controversy. Experiment would be the order of the day seeking to eliminate boredom and fear from the classroom, finding financing through public and private funding. Most important, an open climate would be re-established in a badly split community. Communications between administration, teachers, and community would be continual. The public should know school weaknesses as well as strengths. The people of Berkeley would become full partners in improving public education in Berkeley.

As the Years Pass

On Sept. 10, 1968, four years after Berkeley's secondary schools were racially mixed, every school and most classrooms in the entire system were desegregated. Shortly after that first for a city of more than 100,000 population, Neil V. Sullivan, chief architect and catalyst of total desegregation, left Berkeley to become Commissioner of Education for the Commonwealth of Massachusetts. To his successor, Richard L. Foster, was left the supremely difficult task of leadership in the transformation from mere desegregation to full integration.

Three years have passed. Desegregated Berkeley still survives. It is moving resolutely into 24 alternative or experimental school programs to involve one-third of the entire student body. The new program offers a variety of options to students, teachers, and parents from ethnically separated Black House and La Casa de la Raza to Other Ways, community high schools, schools without walls, traditional programs, ungraded nonstructured programs, multicultural programs, parent-teacher-student managed schools. The twin goals are to destroy institutional racism while providing a vastly improved and contemporary quality of education to each child according to his need and his and his parents' desire.

There seem to be many options to meet the wide variety of needs of teacher as well as student and parent. Yet, at this writing, black, white, Chicano and Asians on staff, in the community, and in the student body are competing for their share of power and opportunity at a time of increasing financial stringency when jobs are scarce and careers hang in the balance. As the days wear on and interracial encounter continues, the people and their leadership will have to meet the challenge of building the deep consensus essential to dividing and sharing the power, rewards, and recognition.

Editor's Note

It may be noted that the process of desegregation of the Berkeley schools has now reached a point where the issue of the need for separate schools for different cultural-ethnic groups (cultural pluralism) is very much to fore. The August 12 Berkeley Daily *Gazette* carried the following article by a staff writer:

Berkeley Schools Segregate in
Efforts to Achieve Integration

The Berkeley public schools are advancing toward the goal of quality integrated education through a kind of segregation: isolating racial groups for special help.

For some, this apparently roundabout maneuver is the only way to achieve mutual ethnic respect and to close the racial academic performance gap.

Casa de la Raza ("house of the race"), Black House, Project Equal One, and other district experimental projects involve education by separation.

They have the unceasing support of the school administration from Supt. Richard Foster on down, and a somewhat apprehensive endorsement from the racially mixed school board.

It is the white liberal board members who have the most trouble comprehending the value of these programs which seem to them at best "risky" and at worst a throwback to southern-style separate-but-equal education.

The message coming from black board members, teachers, and many parents is that de-segregation, "the mere proximity of bodies" has helped neither minority youngsters nor their white peers.

Jesse Anthony, a black music teacher at Columbus School who is an author of Equal One, says his first-hand view of the results of massive cross-town bussing is that it actually reinforces a racial superiority attitude by high-achieving white children toward black youngsters.

And Anthony believes black youth are further damaged by the daily experience of failing to perform on the level of the whites.

Equal One derives it name from the notion that integration is a two-way street in which people must not only respect others, but equally, to respect themselves.

It is a Ford Foundation-supported experimental program for 200 4-6 graders in Columbus School which has a "pull-out" component for one hour of each day during which children may voluntarily meet in a segregated classroom with their ethnic peers.

Modeled after a program in a private San Francisco school, the pull-out period will provide a time for minority youngsters to learn under reduced stress, without the frustrating competition of racially heterogeneous classrooms, Anthony said.

They will receive the individual educational attention they need to learn the basic academic skills without the anxiety of failure, explained Anthony.

"We are seeking equality of ethnic respect and integrity," Anthony said.

Casa and Equal One were given a renewed impetus Tuesday during a special board session during which board president Dr. Samuel Markowitz reversed an earlier board vote which had diminished Casa and all-but annihilated Equal One.

Markowitz had last Thursday joined board members Louise Stoll and Marc Monheimer, all Caucasian, in voting to reduce Casa's staff by one teacher for the fall, and also removing Equal One from an omnibus funding proposal to Ford Foundation.

In making his reversal Tuesday, Markowitz said he was willing to go along with Equal One as "an experiment" that has certain educational risks.

"As a scientist, I'm willing to try this, and if the students perform better on tests of basic skills because of it, I'll be forced to accept the results," Markowitz, a University of California chemist, said after the board session.

He made no comment about his decision to reinstate the Casa

teaching post, but said it was the result of "a person wrestling with his conscience" and was not capitulation to public pressure.

Proponents of the racial "pull-out" projects insist they are not opposing integration or desegregation, and merely wish to strengthen them.

Supt. Foster speaks of a "developing new pluralism" which renders the assimilationistic "racial melting pot" programs obsolete.

Mrs. Stoll who with Monheimer was absent from Tuesday's session, has called the separation programs "immoral, unethical, and illegal."

She said that parents who want such programs for their children can obtain them in neighboring school districts such as Richmond or Oakland, where de-segregation has not been effected.

Monheimer said he agrees in substance with Mrs. Stoll, and is reluctant to turn around from the total integration of classroom concept. (Berkeley Daily *Gazette*, Tuesday, August 12, 1971.)

Mike Culbert, a regular columnist of the *Gazette,* provided these comments excerpted from the August 11 *Gazette:* "Each new ethnic outburst before the deficit-prone and at times chaotic Berkeley Unified School District [BUSD] only indicates how fully BUSD is coming full circle." "For more than a decade, Berkeley liberals planned and moved toward an integrated school system, and Berkeley became the first city of any size to attempt stem-to-stern busing in the interest of desegregation. Now, however, a decentralist attitude is setting in—one which terms the prior thrust toward integration an "earlier concept", and uses the semantics of alternative schools and "alternative modes" to veil the key reality against which the district has been fighting: Perhaps different groups—for whatever reason—learn differently.

"The return to decentralism and the onrush of specialized schools sound suspiciously like neighborhood schools and separate education, the very alleged evils against which the educational desegregationists originally went to war.

"In all the chaos and anarchy of education by quota—and of districts spending themselves silly, as the BUSD has done, on frills and needless capitulations to wave after wave of demands based on anything other than a traditional definition of the word 'education'—there may be some 'goods.'

"Some BUSD programs truly fall into the innovative and creative categories. They have developed despite (or perhaps because of) the tumult and turbulence of the decade of social change that has gone on before.

"There may be new ways to teach people. No one can assume that everything is known about how to teach or the human capacity to learn.

"Sooner or later, however, this or any other school district must resolve the dilemma of whether its primary commitment is to continual experimentation with social change or to equipping students with the essential skills to survive in society—with the foreknowledge that the school does not stand in loco parentis."

The question: To what extent are integration and the new demands for differentiation into separate groups part of a larger process of growth for these groups and the individuals in them?

D.A.

References

1. Berkeley Unified School District, Research and Publications *Student racial census—Fall 1969*; Neil V. Sullivan with Evelyn S. Stewart *Now is the time: Integration in the Berkeley schools.* Bloomington, Indiana: Indiana University Press, 1969. Pp 22-36; Spurgeon Avakian School desegregation in the Berkeley schools. In U.S. Commission on Civil Rights, *Papers prepared on equal opportunities in American cities.* Washington, D.C.: U.S. Govt. Printing Office, 1967. Pp. 101-105; Daniel K. Freudenthal Berkeley high schools integrate, Part II. In Bentley Edwards, et al., *Desegregation in the north.* San Francisco, Cal.: Chandler, 1967. Pp. 50-54.
2. Berkeley Unified School District, Advisory Committee of Citizens *Interracial problems and their effect on education in the public schools of Berkeley, California.* Berkeley, California: The District, October 19, 1959. Pp. 3-5, 6-17; *Berkeley Board of Education Minutes.* January 7, 1958. P. 1; *ibid.*, January 21, 1958. Pp. 1-3; *ibid.*, March 18, 1958. P. 1.
3. Berkeley Unified School District, Advisory Committee of Citizens *op. cit.*, Pp. 18 & 19.
4. Neil V. Sullivan with Evelyn S. Stewart *op. cit.*, Pp. 34-36; Spurgeon Avakian *op. cit.*, Pp. 104-106.
5. Berkeley Board of Education *Minutes.* November 17, 1959. P. 2; *ibid.*, December 1, 1959. Pp. 1, 3-4; *ibid.*, December 15, 1959. Pp. 2-3; *ibid.*, February 2, 1960. Pp. 3-6; *ibid.*, February 16, 1960. Pp. 4-10; *ibid.*, April 5, 1960. Pp. 2-5.
6. Congress of Racial Equality, Berkeley Chapter *Presentation to the Berkeley board of education on de facto segregation.* Berkeley, Cal.: Congress of Racial Equality, 1962.
7. Berkeley Board of Education *Minutes.* March 1, 1960. Pp. 2-7; *ibid.*, March 15, 1960. Pp. 7-11; *ibid.*, June 14, 1960. Pp. 1-4; *ibid.*, June 28, 1960. Pp. 6, 14; *ibid.*, July 19, 1960. p. 7; *ibid.*, August 23, 1960. Pp. 5-9; *ibid.*, November 15, 1960. p. 3; *ibid.*, December 20, 1960. p. 1; *ibid.*, July 3, 1962; *ibid.*, July 17, 1962. p. 5.
8. Neil V. Sullivan with Evelyn S. Stewart *op. cit.*, pp. 41, 42, 45; Berkeley Unified School District *Notes on implementation of the Staats report.* Berkeley, Cal.: The District. February 21, 1961. 7 pp.; Berkeley Unified School District *Improving racial relations in the Berkeley unified school district; Progress and plans.* Berkeley, Cal.: The District. March 20, 1962. 6 pp.; Berkeley Unified School District *Continuing implementation of Staats committee report in 1962 and 1963.* Berkeley, Cal.: The District. 9 pp., Berkeley Board of Education Resolution on de facto segregation. *Minutes.* September 18, 1962. Pp. 3-4; *ibid.*, November 19, 1963. p. 19.
9. Berkeley Board of Education *Minutes.* November 3, 1963. Pp. 14-15.
10. Berkeley Unified School District, Board of Education, Citizens Committee, *De facto segregation in the Berkeley public schools.* Berkeley, Cal.: The District, November 19, 1963. Pp. 28-35.
11. Berkeley Board of Education *Minutes.* November 19, 1963. p. 19; *ibid.*, December 3, 1963. Pp. 1-2, 6-7, 9; *ibid.*, December 17, 1963 Pp. 14-18; Wallace R. Matson "The liberal case against the Hadsell report. In *The Berkeley daily gazette.* December 20, 1963. p. 8.

12. Berkeley Board of Education *Minutes.* December 17, 1963. p. 8; Berkeley Board of Education Public hearing on de facto segregation committee report. *Edison Disc.* January 22, 1964; Berkeley Board of Education *op. cit.,* February 4, 1964. Pp. 6-9; Another 101 comments about Hadsell report. *Berkeley daily gazette.* January 21, 1964. p. 12; Still another 101 comments about Hadsell report. *ibid.,* January 22, 1964. p. 12; 101 comments from Gazette's confidential ballot. *ibid.,* January 20, 1964. p. 12; Wallace R. Matson The liberal case against, Hadsell report. *ibid.,* December 20, 1963. Pp. 8-9.

13. C. H. Wennerberg *Superintendent's report on the staff reaction to the citizens de facto segregation study committee report.* Berkeley, Cal.: Berkeley Unified School District, March 3, 1964. 12 pp. plus appendix on Ramsey Plan.

14. Berkeley Board of Education *Minutes.* March 3, 1964. pp. 6-7, 8-11; *ibid.,* April 7, 1964. Pp. 9-10; Berkeley Unified School District *Task force minutes.* Spring, 1964.

15. Berkeley Unified School District *Desegregation of the Berkeley public schools: Its feasibility and implementation.* Berkeley, Cal.: The School District, May 1964. Pp. 1-4.

16. *ibid.,* pp. 5-25; Berkeley Unified School District Desegregation of the Berkeley Schools. *The superintendent's report of a staff task group study: Appendixes to the report.* Berkeley, Cal.: The School District, May 1964, 112 pp.; Berkeley Board of Education *Minutes.* May 19, 1964. Pp. 11, 13-14, 19-23; *ibid.,* June 2, 1964. Pp. 5-7, Appendix; *ibid.,* June 9, 1964. Pp. 9-11; *ibid.,* June 16, 1964. p. 6.

17. Neil V. Sullivan *A message to the staff.* Berkeley, Cal.: The School District, September 24, 1964.

18. Berkeley Board of Education *Minutes.* October 20, 1964. Pp. 2-3; *ibid.,* May 4, 1965. Pp. 1-4.

19. Berkeley Unified School District, Office of Personnel Director *Minority teacher employment and teacher evaluation as related to concerns expressed by members of the black community.* Berkeley, Cal.: The District, 1968. Bernard Flanagan Progress report—Recruitment of black personnel. *Memorandum to Dr. Neil V. Sullivan.* December 18, 1963. 12 pp.; Berkeley Unified School District, Office of Personnel Director. Berkeley, Cal.: The District, Sept. 21, 1965. Berkeley Unified School District *Racial distribution of classified employees.* Berkeley, Cal.: The District, Revised May 1969.

20. Sullivan, *op. cit.,* pp. 1-4; Berkeley Board of Education *Minutes.* Sept. 1, 1964. Pp. 2-4.

Nine Lessons for the Educational Establishment

(Based on the Integration of the Berkeley Public Schools)

NEIL V. SULLIVAN

Few people in Berkeley knew on the morning of Sept. 10, 1968 that the day was to bring me tremendous personal satisfaction and at the same time result in my decision to leave that community. I had promised a distinguished panel of laymen in the Commonwealth of Massachusetts that I would leave Berkeley if all went well with the final phases of school integration and journey East to become their commissioner of education. As a result, I had mixed emotions on the morning of Sept. 10 as the buses rolled for the first time and thousands of children from kindergarten to grade 6 took their first bus ride to school, and the project that began four years before was to be completed. Mixed emotions because I had Berkeley in my blood—the people, the kids, the teachers, the school board, and, of course, the weather. I had come to Berkeley to integrate the schools, and if all went well on this day, the romance was over. The job was complete, and there were other worlds to conquer.

On Sept. 11, 1968, I received a telegram from Harold Howe, U.S. Commissioner of Education, stating that a new page in history had been written in Berkeley with the complete desegregation of the city schools. On the following day, I visited many of those schools, chatted with students, with members of the Establishment, listened to bus drivers and paraprofessionals, convened a meeting of responsible school officials. The word was the same from all sources: "It had gone extremely well." Was I surprised? Certainly not. The community had spent the better part of two years planning for the total integration of its schools and had indicated its commitment in the most tangible way by almost doubling its tax rate to make certain that integration was done properly, done with style, done with the one thought in mind "to have a school system worthy of imitation and one that was fair to all concerned."

Dr. Sullivan, former Superintendent of the Berkeley Unified School District, is currently Commissioner of Education for the Commonwealth of Massachusetts.

Later that week I announced I was leaving Berkeley to become commissioner of education in Massachusetts as the fifteenth successor to Horace Mann. Now over two years later, I have been asked to journalize briefly in this first issue of the *Community Psychology Monograph Series* what was the significance of the Berkeley experience with particular reference to its effect on the profession as a whole.

I will begin by confessing that at times during the past 20 years, I had about decided that nothing would change the public-school system; we would go on making our little boxes and fitting children (those who fit) into them, carelessly, crudely, and willfully casting adrift any that did not fit the mold. We did not get away with it because young people finally rebelled. They, with leadership first from the black community, then the brown community, blew the whistle. Instead of fitting people into a static social system, they led the movement that is resulting in the restructuring of the total system to meet the needs of all people.

The first lesson I learned in Berkeley, and the one that the teaching profession is now acknowledging, was that the kids were unhappy with the school system and could document the causes for their unhappiness. They knew what they were talking about. They were saying things that few educators fully realized, "that the schools were primarily designed to satisfy the Establishment and not necessarily aimed at meeting the needs of young people." We continued to attempt to prepare all children for a false and unreal college and not for the life they were living.

The word is out in the profession today that the success of the Berkeley project can be traced to student involvement. The Establishment has known for a quarter of a century that teacher involvement is mandatory and for ten years that community participation is essential, but student involvement (all the way into the primary schools) was something most professionals did not consider necessary, proper, or essential for the success of an innovative change in the system. Lesson 1, therefore: involve the kids, all the kids, all the way.

Lesson 2: it can be done. One of the overriding lessons the profession learned from the Berkeley experience is that a community can face the problem of segregation—be torn asunder by it—have recall elections, and still, in fact, pull the community back together again and completely integrate its schools.

Outside of California many educators like to believe that Berkeley succeeded because it did not have the tough dimensions of the problem. They were sure all the black militants lived in Oakland and all the John Birchers were in San Francisco, that the schools were predominantly white and controlled by liberal university professors. Their attitudes changed when they learned that 43% of the Berkeley school population was black, that the Black Panther Party was founded in Berkeley, and that all those "little old ladies in tennis shoes" did not live in Pasadena.

Lesson 3: despite the noise that accompanies any suggestion that school children will be bused, the profession now recognizes that the safest, most efficient way to get children to school is on that school bus. The small neighborhood school, the last bastion of racist America, has failed to educate American children except in isolation, and the cost of operating these "havens of hate" is no longer feasible in most American communities.

Lesson 4: one critical ingredient is needed if integration is to occur, namely a school superintendent who has courage. A committed staff and a school committee with an open mind are needed, but without a superintendent who is willing to push, cajole, motivate, drive with one objective in mind, in short lead, it will not happen. As I look around the country and see the Berkeley model being successfully introduced in communities, I find without exception a school superintendent who has courage to make a decision and to see it through. The fourth lesson, then, is that school desegregation occurs when the superintendent takes the initiative and molds consensus.

Lesson 5: successful school integration costs additional money. I make it abundantly clear to the various public groups I address that retraining of staff, new curriculum material, recruiting black staff and minority staff members generally, improving the school plant must accompany school desegregation. These things cost money. If it is worth doing, it is worth doing well. Promising something better "at the end of the bus ride" is fine, but delivering on this promise is essential. The profession is now aware of the need to sell integration, to explode the myths, to squash rumors if a plan is to be accepted by a community. To gain this acceptance requires a top-notch management team that includes specialists in public relations. You cannot leave it to "George," to the PTA, to the teacher's union, or to the NAACP. You employ skilled technicians who can write, promote, and sell. You use the same techniques that industry uses to sell a new product.

Lesson 6: logistical difficulties do not pose the largest hurdle. Although logistical problems are difficult in many communities, the biggest hurdle is developing the commitment to solve the problem. Once that has been achieved, logistical plans can be developed that will improve the situation in any city.

Lesson 7: the dire consequences predicted for a community that integrates its schools will not occur, particularly if the process of integration is well planned. The Berkeley experience has demonstrated to the profession that integration does not result in an exodus of whites to suburbia. As a matter of fact, the profession is now realizing that the surest way to create such an exodus is to delay integration. The longer that you keep people from working and going to school together, the sooner will they become fearful of each other, and be fertile ground for the rumor and hate mongers. This fear of the unknown will drive both into deeper patterns of segregation that will eventually destroy our cities if not our nation.

Within this lesson, the profession has also learned that public financial support of education can increase when the money is earmarked for equality of opportunity. In Berkeley this occurred during this period, while in Los Angeles and Oakland, suggested tax increases were voted down as these communities sustained the principle of education in isolation. Equally important, we learned that teacher turnover did not accelerate, but rather dropped once the decision was made to integrate.

Lessons 8 and 9: the profession was led to believe before the Berkeley success story unfolded that two results of integration would be (a) increased violence, and (b) white achievement would suffer. The evidence from Berkeley has clearly demonstrated that integration does not dampen or slow down the achievement of middle-class children, that they continue a steady year-by-year achievement gain during the integrated experience. On violence, the schools in Berkely remained calm during the period following the assassination of Martin Luther King and Robert F. Kennedy, while segregated schools throughout the Bay Area and the rest of the country closed their doors. The profession now knows that you bring out the worst in a race, ethnic group, or religious group when you isolate them. Behavior and attitudes and achievement improve when people learn to live together. Although local conditions vary from community to community, the Berkeley experience demonstrates that it is possible for a medium-sized city with a substantial minority population to face the issues of school integration squarely and marshal its resources to work for an effective solution that is fair to all concerned. (You cannot any longer put the onus on the black man. You just cannot close his schools and transport his children.)

The final lesson and perhaps the most significant of all lessons learned in Berkeley was that the best form of compensatory education for minority children, the only one that works, is school integration. We had, along with other educators, poured millions of dollars into remedial programs and purchased all sorts of equipment, had lowered class size, and had done everything possible to stimulate, to challenge, to motivate the minority children. The results of these efforts were generally unsatisfactory. What Berkeley taught the profession in the late '60s was what I had known intuitively for years: the best form of education and one that had worked in America was when rich and poor, black and white learn together in the same educational setting. The minority children, once schools were integrated in Berkeley, have made year-for-year progress in achievement; for the first time, test results indicate that children in the Berkeley schools are achieving above national norms.

Finally, I learned a couple of personal lessons. First, that a change in administration, particularly at the top of the local school system, is healthy and should occur about every five years. One man can move an objective, a program just so far in any given period of time, and a new personality philosophically tuned to change can take over, take a fresh look at the challenge, bring new techniques to cope with the emerging needs, and, as a result, get things moving again. This occurred when I went to Berkeley. It occurred when I left Berkeley.

The second lesson I learned involved the state and how a chief state school officer can help or hinder a local school district bent on effecting progressive change. It was a particularly meaningful lesson, and it still serves as a reminder in my relationships now with school superintendents in Massachusetts.

Unfortunately, such was not the case in California, from the moment I left Prince Edward County and my black Southern brothers, the state superintendent there played the role of antagonist in our efforts to bring equal educational opportunity to the children of Berkeley. The restructuring of that city system has undoubtedly contributed to the restructuring of the entire social system and the former state superintendent could have played a positive role with Berklians in that venture. Instead, he chose to follow a course that, intentionally or not, would have perpetuated a school system static and cancerous, designed for another age, a past generation.

The changes at Berkeley were wrought by men who, following their consciences, made momentous decisions. For my own part, I could do no other; my commitment to the future of America, its dream and promise, was and is total. History will be the final judge of the Berkeley experiment, and I rather think she will judge kindly. Personally, I chose the path of action my conscience dictated. Robert Frost must have faced the crossroads, too. He said it this way:

> "I shall be telling this ages hence
> Perhaps, with many and many a sigh
> Two roads diverged in the woods, and I?—
> I took the road least travelled by
> —And that has made all the difference."

Youth—A View from Berkeley

I. White Youth

ROBERT SCHWEBEL

Through an extensive effort in the past decade, social scientists have established the framework for a serious analysis of modern-day students, youth, and youth activists. Most articles about youth are written from the perspective of "an outsider looking in." Age, identification, disposition, and experiences usually separate the inquirer from the object of study. This is not the case in this article. The topic is psychological and social-science research on white middle-class students, youth, and youth activists, and the old and new directions for psychology indicated by the community psychological services in Berkeley. The perspective is unusual in that the author is in many ways part of the object of study. Bias is inevitable in such a paper, and I will try to be aware of my biases and be objective in my reporting. At the same time, the compensations are twofold. A different perspective on youth is offered, and the biases of the traditional perspective are discussed. Kenneth Keniston, one of the most prominent psychologists involved in the study of youth, has pointed out why bias is inevitable even from sincere social scientists:

> "To discuss today's 'revolting students' is to discuss a controversial political phenomenon, and almost inevitably to make a political statement. Not only outside of scientific circles, but within them, today's student rebels arouse the most intense anxieties, hopes, hostilities, fantasies, and affections. Judgment of these students is inevitably influenced by the writer's psychological, historical, political, and ideological position. The ideal of a completely 'value free' social science, psychoanalysis, or other form of inquiry is illusory, and especially illusory when dealing with controversial current topics [Keniston, 1970, p. 7].

There is a tendency to obscure and mystify serious social problems and the

---

Mr. Schwebel is a graduate student at the University of California, Berkeley. Cynthia Kristensen and Daniel Adelson helped with the paper.

need for social change in the psychological research on youth, especially on youth activism. This is illustrated by the often undifferentiated definition of alienation in the literature and by the philosophy of a functionally stable society that underlies a good deal of psychological thought. It can also be seen in the two dominant forms of psychological commentary on activism: one that reduces it to nothing but presumed intrapsychic origins, and the other that seeks to understand it strictly in terms of the personality factors of the activists and/or the internal dynamics of their families.

Youth Alienation
and the Philosophy of the Functional Stability of Society

Although there is great flexibility in the definition of alienation in the literature, it is striking to notice how often alienation is described as a form of deviancy or treated as if it meant the same thing as deviancy (Gould, 1969; Whittaker & Watts, 1969; Tannenbaum, 1969). Confusion seems to result because the word alienation is employed as if it referred to the behavior by people who do not follow the dominant values of society. When used this way, alienation becomes almost synonymous with "deviancy." This usage fails to discriminate between people who consciously analyze society and as a result either confront it or withdraw from it and people who "get bounced from wall to wall" with little control over their fate. The philosophy that underlies this failure in discrimination is of a society that is functionally stable, or, as Seymour Martin Lipset proclaims, is "the end of ideology" and the achievement of "stable democracy." Tom Bottomore explains:

> "The essential idea upon which it rests is that every society should be conceived as a system in equilibrium; and that any disturbance of this equilibrium should be seen as provoking a responsive adaptation in the various subsystems of society so that equilibrium is restored and the society is maintained in its original, or slightly modified, form. This idea found its strongest expression in that version of functionalism in which the force that brings about equilibrium, adaptation, and integration is defined as a 'central value system'; that is, a set of fundamental values, presumed to be accepted by all or most members of a society, which determine the form of each particular social system. [1970, p. 20]."

Bottomore points out that this theory creates in its adherents "an extreme insensitivity to the potentialities for change in human society," and that it encourages "a propensity to regard the fleeting present as an eternal order."

Reductionist Theories of Activism

An analysis of youthful "rebellion," "alienation," and "activism" (often indiscriminately lumped together) follows from the premise of a functionally stable society that reduces these forms of behavior in young people to peculiar, pathological, perverse, or unreasonable motivations, motivations that are unworthy of expression and must be controlled. It should be noted that this variety of social thought comes predominantly from the armchair—not from rigorous research—and, despite the general absence of data and studies, that it has gained support from large segments of the population.

Lewis Feuer (1969) explains student activism primarily in terms of the unconscious forces of generational struggle. He conceives of student activists as largely motivated by unconscious drives to revolt against the deauthoritized father. According to Feuer, student activists overcome the guilt of generational revolt—of the would be parricide—by demonstrating they are selfless and winning the comforting maternal love of the oppressed. They do this by joining social movements that fuse their feelings of guilt with their altruistic and overly idealistic feelings. However,

> "Where such an imposition of a student movement on the process of social change has taken place, the evidence is overwhelmingly that the chances for a rational evolution and achievement of social goals have been adversely affected [Feuer, 1969, p. 8]."

Feuer believes that student movements echo the trauma of adolescence and inevitably involve generational conflicts. Thus he feels that the movements must always disintegrate into disorderly, irrational, and self- and other-destructive actions. This negative evaluation applies to Feuer's perspective of activism on the campuses: "Indeed, we may affirm the generalization: wherever student movements have flourished, academic freedom has consequently declined [1969, p. 44]."

Dwight McDonald wrote about the position (which he does not share) of a very prominent psychologist who falls in the reductionist category:

> "Bruno Bettleheim is convinced that the more extreme of young militants are raging against a chaos that is within themselves, not the world. 'While consciously they demand freedom and participation, unconsciously their commitment to Mao and leaders like him suggests their desperate need for controls from the outside, since without them they cannot bring order to their inner chaos.' To the criticism that Dr. Bettleheim is insensitive to social injustices and the imperviousness of social institutions, Bettleheim replies: 'One should go along with the Establishment if it is halfway reasonable; any

> establishment is only halfway reasonable.' And he returns to his
> conviction that 'the militant is more motivated by his inner anger
> than by the wrongs of society . . .' [1970, pp. 22-23] ."

If "any establishment is only halfway reasonable," then it is implied that anyone who tries to transform it is unreasonable, perhaps neurotic, and certainly wasting time. In his position, Bettleheim only slighly diverges from the view of the functionally stable society. This view that any society inevitably frustrates its young has been offered in a variety of contexts (Hall, 1904, Vol. 2, pp. 71-72; Parsons, 1962; Erikson, 1970).

Freudian interpretation is probably the most common reductionist theory of student activism. The argument usually postulates Oedipal origins for the rage and revolt of students against existing institutions and values, and either implicitly or explicitly seeks to explain student protest as "nothing but" its presumed intrapsychic roots. Keniston has criticized the psychoanalytic position:

> "The usefulness of the Oedipus Complex in explaining political and
> historical phenomena is open to challenge. In attempting to
> understand student revolt, we are of course not attempting to
> understand a universal phenomenon. Rather, we are seeking to
> explain why at a particular time in modern history (but not at other
> times), a particular group of young men and women (but not most
> of their contemporaries) have become intensely concerned with the
> social and political injustices of their world, have devised a new
> series of tactics, strategies and interpretations of reality, and have set
> themselves against established institutions and values. . . . Yet if the
> Oedipus Complex is a universal developmental phenomenon, Oedipal
> feelings alone are of little use in accounting for specific groups acting
> in specific ways at specific historical moments [1970, p. 6] ."

Lewis Mayhew (1968), in the Freudian tradition, suggests that "the drive to campus power sublimates guilt" (i.e., guilt in students about affluence and guilt for not yet having attained adult status).

> "The problem of affluence is intensified by the plight of minority
> groups in America and by the War in Vietnam. . . . The protesting
> college student may well be compensating for his knowledge that if a
> war-based economy had not made his parents affluent he might be
> fighting the war instead of attending college. Police billy clubs are
> still safer than Vietcong grenades and he knows it [p. 49] ."

The reductionist theories of activism attempt to discredit the sincerity of young people and the validity of their actions through psychological explanation of real social concerns. It seems that in some instances the very minimum prerequisite for writing about activism—human contact with activists—has not been met. The inherent danger in this type of commentary is that society may try simply to stop protest without listening to what young people have to say. The logical extension of this mode of thought is the act of political repression. When Vice President Agnew (cited in Stark, 1970) says that college campuses are "circus tents or psychiatric centers for over-privileged, under-disciplined, irresponsible children of well-to-do permissivists," then we should listen to Keniston (1970), who warns that

> "This body of work (psychological reductionism of youth activism) while far from consistent, is beginning to provide intellectual respectability and ideological underpinning for the rejection and even repression of student protest."

Socialization Correlates and Personality Factors in Youth Activists

Over the past six years an impressive amount of research appeared on the socialization correlates and personality factors in young activists and in alienated youth. This is the other mode of thought that has dominated the research on activist and alienated youth. A review of this literature can be found in a chapter by Block, Haan, and Smith (1968). This research relies heavily on questionnaires, interviews, and personality inventories in portraying the family backgrounds and personality configurations of activists.

Berkeley Youth Portrayed

Probably because Berkeley has been the center for the development of youth subcultures and student activism, a number of studies on these topics have been done in Berkeley with Berkeley youth as subjects. This research provides a picture of youth activists and youth subcultures in general, but more specifically it provides a picture of certain aspects of Berkeley youth.

Smith, Haan, and Block (1970) used Berkeley residents (and San Francisco residents from across the Bay) as subjects. The experimenters developed a typology to differentiate youth based on the dual criteria of degree of involvement with contemporary political-social issues and the degree of acceptance or rejection of the traditional values and the institutional authority of the society. Typological classification is established by degree of participation in social-service activities (such as volunteer work in hospitals, schools, and social agencies, or work with the handicapped); degree of participation in protest (picketing, demonstrating, peace marches, civil-rights work); and membership in fraternity or sorority group. In all, there are five typological groups, two of them—activists and dissenters—are discussed below. (The discussion is limited to differences that discriminate significantly over all five groups.)

In this categorization, activists and dissenters are both designated as being involved in two or more protest activities. Neither activists nor dissenters are members of fraternities or sororities. They are differentiated in the area of social service. Activists have participated in one or more social-service activities while dissenters have not. In addition to activists and dissenters, there are three more conservative typologies.

In self-descriptive adjective Q sorts, activist men regarded themselves as especially rebellious, restless, informed, and assertive; the activist women regarded themselves as rebellious, restless, perceptive, worrying, and uncompromising. The male dissenters were especially likely, when compared with members of other groups, to call themselves idealistic, perceptive, individualistic, curious, critical, and self-centered, while their counterparts among the women regard themselves as especially individualistic, informed, and open and frank.

In another publication, Block, Haan & Smith (1969) summarized two of their heavily emphasized findings about the socialization of activists and dissenters (based on retrospective child rearing adjective Q sorts given to the youth).

> "Perhaps not surprisingly, the Dissenters were found to be more frequently in rebellion against the political-social ideologies of their parents than were the Activists [p. 174] .
>
> "The second distinction to be made between the Activists and Dissenters involves the notion of permissiveness and its applicability to the parental child-rearing orientations of the activists. When the descriptions of student protesters' parents are compared with the stereotype of permissiveness ascribed to these parents by the lay press, it is apparent that the newspaper interpretation is reasonably correct in regard to the Dissenters' origins but is quite wrong regarding the Activists. [p. 175] ."

Kathleen Mock and Paul Heist (1969) gathered data about potential activists from students at the University of California at Berkeley (and from two other campuses of the university). They defined "potential activists" as that 5% of the entering freshmen class of 1965 who were "favorable and supportive" toward the Berkeley Free Speech Movement (FSM) of the year before. After a period of a year, retesting indicated that the great majority of the potential-activist sample had retained their favorable attitude toward the FSM.

Mock and Heist found that the personalities of the potential activists predisposed them toward serious scholarship. As freshmen they exhibited values and orientations that generally lead to graduate study. Their scores on the Omnibus Personality Inventory (OPI) suggest they were involved in the world of ideas and aesthetics, and had attained a degree of freedom in their thinking that enabled them to deal with issues of philosophy and ethics. On social-emotional scales of the OPI, they were much more like the average college student.

The social-economic origins of the potential-activist students were chiefly upper middle class. Their fathers were primarily white-collar employees and earned at least $12,000 annually. Although the parents' religious affiliations were mainly Protestant or Jewish, most of the students had pulled away from the beliefs and practices of traditional religion.

There were important differences between the potential activists and the rest of the sample selected from students who entered in 1965. On personality measures the potential activists were more highly motivated toward intellectual pursuits, more independent in judgments, and more likely to express impulses and feelings. Politically, the parents of pro-FSM students were more liberal than parents of other students. Nevertheless, there was greater disparity between the political positions of pro-FSM students and their parents than between the political positions of students in other groups and their parents.

Watts, Whittaker, and Lynch have compared activist students, a random sample of students, and the noncomformist disaffiliated youth (non-students) in Berkeley. The nonstudents consist of collegiate-age youth (and their older counterparts) who are neither formally enrolled at the university nor members of the conventional work force, but who gravitate to the university campus area and live a marginal existence.

In one study Watts and Whittaker (1968) profiled the nonstudents. It was found that the nonstudents come from families of similar socioeconomic backgrounds to the random sample of students. The young nonstudents are alienated from their families as well as from society. Though oriented toward creative fields, they are less interested in a career than their student counterparts. They are not political in the conventional sense; but, in spite of sometimes disavowing any hope for social change, they still turn out for protest activities more often that the random student sample. The nonstudent group is comparable in ability to college students and perceives the functions of the university in a somewhat similar manner. The disaffiliates, however, are extremely dissatisfied with higher education.

Watts, Lynch, and Whittaker (1969) found that both the activist group and the nonstudent group scored high on a scale of anomie. Whereas the nonstudents were estranged from their families, however, the activists were not. The nonstudents were cut off from their families in terms of values related to intellectual, religious, and political beliefs, life styles, and future goals. The nonstudents' families did not differ from the families of the random sample of students. These data suggest that whether or not a young person becomes an activist or becomes disaffiliated may be related to whether or not the parents' values are consistent with the child's. However, no causality is indicated in these correlational findings, and the nonstudent's estrangement from his family may be a recent product of his disaffiliation from society.

Problems with research on socialization and personalities of activists

The research on the socialization and personalities of activists has had the effect of disclosing the humanity and sincerity of youth, and serves as a valuable rebuttal against arguments for repression. In fact, Bay (1967) pointed out that probably the most consistent finding in this research is that student activists and student liberals show greater intellectual ability, higher intellectual disposition, and better academic performance than their less liberal and less activist counterparts. However, there are two very serious problems associated with the research that provides a preliminary picture of some psychological characteristics of activists. It is ironic that at the same time these descriptive studies can be used as an argument against repression, they can also be used as part of a repressive technique. The knowledge acquired through these studies is beginning to provide a basis for locating or isolating activists or potential activists through background investigations or personality inventories. At a time when schools prematurely locate "intelligent children" and then bestow special privileges on them through such mechanisms as the tracking system and the self-fulfilling prophecy, and President Nixon speaks of locating potential criminals in their childhood so that the government can intervene, one must be wary of the potential applications of descriptive studies that locate significant and important critics of society and agents of change—activists.

A second major problem with research on the socialization and personalities of activists rests in the limited viewpoint of studying a broad social issue, activism, from the narrow standpoint of psychology. Social problems, values, and issues directly connected with activism tend to become buried in research, which gives the mystifying impression that student activism can be thoroughly understood through an analysis of personality factors and the internal dynamics of the family. This research on the one hand obscures serious social problems and on the other hand implies that an evaluation of social action can be made independent of a social analysis.

A question frequently raised and often contradictorily answered in the literature on the characteristics of youth activists has been whether the values of the young activists are continuous or discontinuous with the values of their parents (Flacks, 1967; Friedenberg, 1969; Grinder, 1969; Keniston, 1969). In other words, have the young activists accepted the values of their parents or are they rebelling against them? The question seems to be a minor variation from the one that asks, Is it true that activism is caused by Oedipal rebellion? The mystification lies in the implication that the worthiness of protest can somehow be determined by studying the family relationships. That is, if youth are rebelling against their parents' values, then they are simply involved in that stage of life when they rebel against their parents' values, and their rebellion can be dismissed. Or, if they are not rebelling simply against their parents' values, then they can be taken seriously. The judgment of whether or not youth activists are to be taken seriously, however, should be made on the basis of what they do.

Further, to say that activists either tend to be or tend not to be in rebellion against their parents' values is a grossly oversimplified way of understanding the psychological qualities of the complex behavior of activism.

Preoccupation with the question of whether or not youth are rebelling against their parents seems to have created a situation of 'not seeing the forest for the trees.' The study of a basically social issue (activism)—the relationship of man and woman to society—in almost purely psychological terms tends to obscure the social reality under investigation. Sometimes it appears that young activists and their parents share similar values because they both say they want the same things. Keniston wrote that "Activists are *not*, on the whole, repudiating or rebelling against explicit parental values and ideologies. On the contrary, there is some evidence that such students are living out their parents' values in practice ... [1967, p. 119]." In American society, just about everybody will verbally favor peace, freedom, and democracy. It is, however, uncritical to assume that all Americans share these values. There are great differences between those who espouse a set of values and practice them and those who espouse the same values and do not practice them or practice values that are in reality quite different. (Consider, for example, the different values held by the peace movement and by Nixon, who claims to be for peace.) It is probably an obliviousness to the differences between practiced and preached values that leads Flacks (1967, p. 54) to state that "there is no evident erosion of the legitimacy of established authority; we do not seem, at least on the surface, to be in a period of rapid disintegration of traditional values." By studying the psychological aspects of activism without putting it into a social context, only a preliminary, peripheral, and surface correlational understanding is possible.

In much of the personality and socialization literature the protests of white middle-class youth are seen to originate in the rational analysis, idealism, high values, and insight that this group is said to possess (Bay, 1967; Flacks, 1967; Keniston, 1967; Trent & Craise, 1967). It is suggested that society is really meeting their needs, but that these young people are so bright and have such high values nurtured in them that they still want to improve the world more. This contrasts with the picture presented in the scientific journals of black youth protesting from anger and frustration. Accounting for protest without indicating that rational thought and high values play a role in black rebellion and that anger and frustration play a part in white rebellion seems to contribute less to an understanding of dissent than to the propagation of stereotyped thought about the races. From the white perspective, it can be seen that social conditions that foster anger and frustration will tend to be obscured.

An article by Flacks (1967) on the roots of student protest is an example of how conditions that foster anger and frustration in white youths tend to be obscured. He hypothesizes that student unrest in white upper-middle-class schools reflects the conflict between a personality type emerging from a style of child rearing and an educational process that is increasingly rationalized and depersonalized. He suggests that the liberal family relationships of the upper middle-class create youth who "are likely to be particularly sensitized to acts of arbitrary authority, to unexamined expressions of allegiance to conventional values, to instances of institutional practices which conflict with expressed ideals [p. 61]." He reports that upper-middle-class student protesters at the University of Chicago have indeed experienced liberal child rearing and that they have high levels of four primary values that differentiate them from their fellow students: aesthetic and emotional sensitivity, intellectualism, humanitarianism, and personal flexibility. By the end of the article, the activists are portrayed as very sensitive and intelligent people who have perhaps expected too much from their school. The rationalization and depersonalization of education, which is mentioned in the beginning of the article, is not considered an important factor creating anger and frustration; it has become almost irrelevant. Flacks wrote:

> "The research reported here emphasizes family socialization and other antecedent experiences as determinants of student protest, and leads to the prediction that students experiencing other patterns of early socialization will be unlikely to be in revolt. This view needs to be counterbalanced by recalling instances of active student unrest on campuses where very few students are likely to have the backgrounds (white, upper middle class) suggested here as critical. Is it possible that there are two components to the student protest movement—one generated to a great extent by early socialization; the second by grievances indigenuous to the campus [presumably at poor and black schools] [p.73]."

Activism: Psychological and Social Determinants

Psychologists have engaged in an extensive endeavor to understand and evaluate youth activism by studying the intrapsychic and family lives of activists. Activism, however, is a complex behavior generated by a combination and interaction of personality factors and social problems. As long as only psychological factors are considered and until the interaction is studied, research on activism will remain at a superficial level. You cannot expect that by asking Dwight Eisenhower about his childhood or by administering a personality inventory to him that you could make generalizations about the qualities of World War II. If activism, protest, and young people are to be understood and if the quality of life for young people is to be improved, then a crucial first step will be to take seriously what young people articulate about how they are experiencing the world.

In part the insensitivity to social problems in youth literature reflects the general trend in psychology that pretends to explain serious social problems *strictly* in terms of psychological mechanisms. This approach suggests that genetic makeup and childhood experiences explain failure in school, that achievement motivation explains impoverishment or unemployment, and that the subconscious desires of women explain unwanted pregnancies. By this approach, sexism, racism, economic exploitation, and the quality of schools and other institutions remain unquestioned. Social problems are defined away as problems within an individual or within a family. Social scientists often do not seem to recognize that this society fails to meet the needs of large numbers of people. Perhaps this blindness results from the limitations inherent in the homogeneity of social scientists, most of whom view the world from the perspective of a social group that has its own needs met.

The two predominant theoretical approaches to youth and activism in the mainstream social-science research publications are (a) reductionism (activism can best be understood in terms of personality factors and intrapsychic mechanisms about which the author usually has speculated) and (b) personality and socialization studies (activism can best be understood in terms of personality factors in light of family dynamics). There is a third major theory that rarely appears in the mainstream social-science research journals. It is the theory of the worldwide youth movement. This theory is that activism is caused by oppression. Alienation is the result of people being unaware of their oppression and therefore unable to act against it (activism is best understood in terms of personality factors in light of family dynamics, in light of society dynamics). The city of Berkeley has agencies and organizations that have adopted, in practice, the three predominant theories of activism and youth (the two that are reviewed above and the third that is espoused by the worldwide youth movement). Psychological services rarely adopt reductionist theories unless the service offered is required and not optional to youth, although certain aspects of the reductionist theories sometimes unwittingly enter into their practice. The Berkeley Police Department and the local newspaper, however, have adopted the reductionist theory. The community psychological services are interesting mixtures of the other two theories of youth. Often it is hard to distinguish the two and find out whether a large social picture is truly part of the service offered to youth. When reading about the organizations in the following pages it is interesting to note the degree to which the organizations allow the larger social context to enter into their programs.

Browning (1970) wrote that during the past six years the Berkeley Police Department changed in character from a liberal one to a repressive one. It has publicized and experimented with a vast array of armaments for fighting political demonstrations, and it has gained a reputation among the young as a force that constantly harasses, busts, and intimidates youth. Just last year the city council only narrowly defeated a proposal to arm the department with a helicopter. Meanwhile, the Berkeley Gazette expressed its opinion. The following option was called for in an editorial that appeared on July 22, 1970:

"It is making Berkeley a "hot town"—yanking back the welcome mat, as it were. A continual vigilance of hitchhikers, and the utterly necessary crackdown on the young are excellent starts in this direction. . . . But the pressure must be kept up—with the full understanding that those elements which feel most alluded to in the crackdown will retaliate on a scale equal to their desperation."

In sharp contrast are organizations that at least provide youth with some specific service or an opportunity to get together and talk about themselves. These organizations flow from the studies of youth personalities and socialization characteristics. Youth are seen as struggling individuals who are entitled to assistance in working out problems (often of identity). It is assumed that they can be understood in strictly psychological terms to the exclusion of a well-articulated social perspective. These organizations offer youth some service or an opportunity to talk, with a heavy emphasis placed on the psychological aspects of themselves to the point of obscuring serious underlying social issues. A number of community psychological services in Berkeley fall in this category.

It can be seen that the theoretical position that the rate of widespread social change has caused problems in youth is directly related to research that seeks psychological explanations for more complex social issues. This theory in its generality fails to come to terms with social problems and with the problem of social deterioration. It implies that the feelings of loneliness or alienation or problems of identity are psychological by-products of people who have failed to keep pace with progress. They are not seen as psychological problems demanding a social context, as interactional problems between a sick society and the personality of an individual. What is really a social problem defining a youth problem is perceived as a youth problem defining a social problem. A number of community psychological services in Berkeley use this theoretical orientation.

Berkeley now has community psychological services that are an outgrowth of the worldwide youth movement. The three main themes of the youth activism have been a call for self-determination by all peoples, an end to exploitation and its replacement by reciprocal relationships, and the creation of a new culture that reflects the preceding values. The seriousness of these demands is reflected in the recent history of Berkeley, which has been shaped to a large extent by its young inhabitants. Berkeley had its first protest against the war in Viet Nam in March 1963. Less than a year later the Free Speech Movement marked the beginning of campus unrest throughout the country. Since then, draft resistance, the Free University system, and the underground press started in Berkeley. In addition, there have been a rent strike within the city and a Third World strike at the university. The famous People's Park was built by Berkeley youth. In April 1971 a vote will be taken about the issue of Community Control of Police. (Ed.'s note: Community control failed in the April election though a radical slate was elected to the city council.) A petition is now circulating that would put a referendum on the same ballot authorizing the city of Berkeley to sign a peace treaty with the people of Viet Nam. The War Crimes Tribunal continues at the university. Within this context, new types of community psychological services are developing in Berkeley in which there are no power hierarchies, in which people are not doing something for others but with them, in which people are allowed to understand their problems in a social context, in which the organizers are radical, in which young people define their own needs, and in which policy comes from those who are served. A few of these organizations are discussed in the pages that follow.

The assumption of "The Bridge" is that the system that breeds addiction can never get at the root problem and cure it.

> "Our basic thesis answers to a need for developing our own organic-cultural means to deal with problems that cannot be solved prior to the imminent demise of the death culture [Free University of Berkeley, Fall Catalog, 1970]."

The program is conceived of as a counterculture alternative for the junkie who has internalized the "death instinct and destructiveness of American culture." Methadone maintenance programs are seen as a political panacea in which the addict substitutes one addiction for another. Synanon-structured programs are seen as fostering strict interpersonal dependency relationships and as inhibiting the actualization of a sense of personal autonomy. To build the "new cultural person," a number of programs, some of them still in the planning stages, have been proposed: radical group process sessions; the training of individuals in various skills and crafts (such as carpentry, leatherwork, organic medicine, organic farming); referrals to appropriate services of local hospitals; and the availability of "rap sessions" on a 24-hour basis.

Community Psychology: Youth Serving Institutions

Project Community

A new social institution being developed and researched in Berkeley is Project Community. It evolved conceptually and physically out of therapeutic explorations with adolescent "drug abusers" carried on in research and training programs at the Psychology Clinic of the University of California. As the program has developed the drug issue became connected with more central concerns. Project Community is now seen as

> "a youth serving institution in which drug abuse is one of the central, though by no means exclusive, concerns. . . . Project Community is self-consciously an education institution, but one whose primary concern is to help young people explore seriously the question of how to live a life [Korchin & Soskin, 1970]."

Project Community is oriented toward self-exploration. The core of the program for self-exploration is carried on through what is called a "primary group."

> "The principal objective of the primary group is to create a small stable human unit in which members can, over time, explore the difficult and often painful, yet sometimes exhilaratingly rewarding process of coming to know oneself and to understand one's impact on other people [Korchin & Soskin, 1970]."

Primary groups consist of eight to ten young people and two adult staff members meeting weekly in 1½-hour discussions. Complementing the primary groups are programs in encounter, self-awareness, meditation, body awareness, and "guided daydreaming." In all these programs, the emphasis is on getting to know oneself and to know others. In this age of confusion and isolation, Project Community offers a stable community, a sense of belonging, a sense of family, and a place to make contact. As one participant put it: "My family is just too small for my feelings."

The Free Church

Perhaps the most active community psychological service in Berkeley has been the Free Church, founded by local churches of six denominations in 1967. It is an urban mission of the Diocese of California and the Executive Council of the Episcopal Church, the Synod of Golden Gate, and the Board of the National Missions of the Presbyterian Church. The Free Church serves many of the traditional religious functions, though usually in innovative ways. In its less religious aspects, the Free Church is an

> "ecumenical community in Berkeley:—Serving the needs of youth, street people, students, and alienated adults in the South Campus Area, who are a part of the emerging 'counter-culture' in America.—Planning and carrying out concrete actions, to turn people against racism, militarism, and pollution, and to push forward the loving revolutions of justice, peace and ecology [Berkeley Free Church, booklet, undated]."

The hub of the Free Church's activities is the Berkeley Switchboard, which was the second installation of what is becoming a growing national network of switchboards. Nearly 160 trained volunteers take calls ranging from inquiries about legal aid, draft help, and drug abuse to threats of suicide and requests for assistance from hysterical parents of runaways. Switchboard operators make medical and psychiatric referrals and offer information on birth control and pregnancy problems, community events, transportation, and draft or military problems. In addition, the switchboard serves as a rumor-control center during community crisis and often as the first place people call when they are arrested. The Free Church estimates that they receive as many as 900 calls per week. Policy for the operation of the switchboard is made in a collective manner:

"Most of our volunteers are members of the very community which Switchboard serves—for ours is a ministry *with* and *of,* not to young people. The volunteers as a whole make up the Switchboard Collective' meeting regularly for study, planning and policy making. The management of this service rotates weekly among the volunteers [Berkeley Free Church, booklet, undated] ."

Housing and travelers' aid is a second major function of the Free Church. In particular it serves the needs of an ever increasing hitchhiking circuit. The Free Church helps these travelers by providing information on community resources, a mail and message service, a free-meal program, a checking and storage service for backpacks, and a crash-pad program (from November 1969 to November 1970 over 7,000 transient people were housed in Berkeley by this program).

Another major service of the Free Church is counseling of all sorts. "Because we are hip, young people will turn in trust to us, where they are distressful (sometimes for very good reason) of established churches and agencies [Berkeley Free Church, booklet, undated] ."

Still another function of the church has been that of community organizing.

"The Church which insists on designing and running services for its community which treat only the symptoms of a sick society is in danger of keeping an indigent population to serve. This is colonialism. Free Church, on the other hand, sees as a large part of its job the task of organizing the community to serve itself [Berkeley Free Church, booklet, undated] ."

The Free Church facilitated or helped organize the Barkeley Community Health Project (the Free Clinic and RaP Center), the Berkeley Runaway Center, the free-meal program, the ACLU Police Complaint Center, and the Youth Coalition for Self-Defence (legal aid to juveniles and "street people").

The Free Church helps in Movement work.

"Free Church is a community committed to getting at the core of youth alienation. We see the function of the Church to be the Servant of the Movement [Berkeley Free Church, booklet, undated] ."

The Free Church has been active in the antiwar and draft-resistance movement. It supported the People's Park development, and after the police attack it operated a hospital for injured demonstrators and helped raise bail funds. It provided street medics during numerous police-youth confrontations, led the opposition to the Berkeley Police Department's plan for helicopter surveillance, and is active in supporting the Community Control of Police initiative on the April ballot. The political analysis of the Free Church follows:

"When youth are more and more treated as an oppressed class and students are massacred on campuses like Kent and Jackson, and teargassed from helicopters in Berkeley, the Church must speak out clearly against this escalation of violence and oppression. Free Church has become, in fact, the Church for the Movement in Berkeley. We witness within it the non-violence of Jesus, but know that in the end there can be no peace without freedom. We see our job primarily to be that of speaking to the far more dangerous violence of war, racism, oppression, and passive acquiescence to injustice.

There are consequences which come from being a church witnessing for social change: Free Church has been tear-gassed twice, both Jock [Resident Theologian, Jock Brown] and Dick [the Reverend Dick York] have been seriously beaten by police, several of our staff have been arrested, we have had bullets shot through our office windows, and two bomb threats. But then we are taught to expect that, aren't we?"

Church is perhaps the most established of all establishment institutions. The Free Church has shown that established institutions can truly serve young people in a radical way. This is evident in its radical redefining of function illustrated by: its switchboard, which has its policy set by the community members who make it up; its overall radical analysis of the society and dedication to radical change; its acceptance of young people and desire to serve them in ways they define; its efforts to help the community organize around what the community perceives as its needs; its existence as part of, and not external to the community; in short its faithfulness to Christian values.

Community Psychology: Special Services

Bridge over Troubled Waters

Berkeley has, of course, moved toward establishing a community mental-health program with both direct and indirect services through the use of government funding. A variety of services have also arisen that have no or little government support. One of these is a program for heroin addicts called "Bridge over Troubled Waters." A variety of new types of service have also arisen that have no or little government support. The program, though started less than one year ago, is already in severe trouble. An ex-addict working for the program said that the problem is that people "don't know and don't think" about heroin addiction. Program developers feel that heroin addiction is a problem that the government defines and that the people accept unquestioningly. In fact, tha government founder, in a newspaper interview, said that the government uses heroin to "justify everything it wants to about law."

Therapy and Encounter

Personal Exploration Groups (PEG)

In the summer of 1966 a young minister put up posters around Berkeley announcing groups that would do something about the problems of alienation. Originally the groups were seen as a family or a small community in which members could experience a sense of belonging and commitment. By word of mouth increasing numbers of people heard about and came to groups. Participants gradually developed group-leadership skills. The idea of "encounter" crystallized, and experienced leaders began training new people in basic Rogerian principles and encounter techniques.

Groups in this program have come to be called "Personal Exploration Groups" (PEG), and up to 1970 over 5,000 people have been in them. Each academic quarter 30 to 40 groups of 12 members each are arranged. They meet for an evening session once a week for ten weeks and have a weekend retreat. A $500,000 grant from the Research Division of the Department of Health, Education, and Welfare and a small fee for group participants keep the program financially solvent.

The Rap Center

The brutal beatings endured by demonstrators at People's Park motivated a number of concerned individuals to learn the art of the medic. In response to a perceived community need, and in anticipation of an influx of young people in the summer of 1969, this group of skilled medics, joined by other community residents, established the Free Medical Clinic in Berkeley. Within a month talk began about establishing a psychological service to complement the medical one. The name RaP Center, from Radical Psychiatry, was selected to designate the new service. Claude Steiner, who conceptualized many of the basic principles of the RaP center, summarized them:

"1. No medical control, and the rejection of medical terminology. 2. Determination of competence via observation of work only. 3. The assumption that disordered behavior is largely the result of disordered relationships and environment leading to the use of groups as the ideal context for study and change. 4. The rejection and disuse of diagnostic labels and their replacement by description of behavior. 5. The belief that deviant behavior is a person's right . . . Thus all services should be contractual, that is, it should have clear cut goals agreed upon by the person and the psychiatrist. 6. The complete openness about records, staff discussion and decisions, and the avoidance of one way observation or communication [Steiner, 1970b, p. 5]."

Functionally there are three main components of the program: contact rap, heavy rap, and training rap. Contact rap takes the place of the intake or screening interview at most psychiatric services and serves as the hub of the program. When an individual comes to the RaP Center he joins a contact rap—a group of people talking—in which the individual can just rap and/or learn how to get involved in any other of the activities at the RaP Center he desires. If it is just contact and rapping that he wants, then the individual attends contact raps. If the individual wants to work on a personal problem, then a heavy rap group—a problem-solving therapy group meeting regularly—is recommended. If the individual wants to seriously dedicate himself to work in the RaP Center, then a training rap is designated.

Although the RaP Center was radical in its criticism of traditional psychiatry and progressive in its orientation and organization, at first a radical theory of psychiatric practice was lacking. Filling the void have been the more liberal and progressive aspects of the traditional therapies (groups, contracts, problem-solving approach, plus an eclectic selection of other approaches). Currently the RaP Center serves as a liberal institution where people can get psychiatric services at no cost. Some 150 people, mostly of the young or street-people variety, are served weekly. Policy decisions at the RaP Center are arrived at by all staff and nonstaff people who have been participating in the activities of the RaP Center for at least a month. The center's financial support has come entirely from the community through donations and benefits. Resistances have been many. Recently the Bureau of Adjustment almost voted the Free Clinic and RaP Center out of the city. During a local riot the police launched a vicious attack on the Free Clinic and RaP Center, destroying medical supplies and clubbing doctors, patients, and staff alike.

Radical Psychiatry

Psychiatry is the art of soul healing. Because it is felt that the medical practice of psychiatry is a step sideways rather than forward from the state of the art in the middle ages, a radical change is indicated. Claude Steiner (1970a), a Berkeley psychologist who had been involved in the struggle over People's Park and instrumental in starting the RaP Center, together with Hogie Wycoff, who had been active in the women's movement, provided a basic theoretical position for the radical practice of psychiatry.

"The first principle of radical psychiatry is that in the absence of oppression, human beings will, due to their basic nature or soul, which is preservative of themselves and their species, live in harmony with nature and each other. Oppression is the coercion of human beings by force or threats of force, and is the source of all human alienation.

"The condition of the human soul which makes soul healing necessary is alienation. Alienation is a feeling within a person that he is not part of the human species, that she is dead or that everyone is dead, that he does not deserve to live or that someone wishes her to die. . . . Alienation is the essence of all psychiatric conditions. This is the second principle of radical psychiatry. Every psychiatric diagnosis except for those that are *clearly* organic in origin is a form of alienation.

"The third principle of radical psychiatry is that all alienation is the result of oppression about which the oppressed has been mystified or deceived. By deception is meant the mystification of the oppressed into believing that she is not oppressed or that there are good reasons for her oppression. The result is that the person instead of sensing his oppression and being angered by it decides that his ill feeling are his own fault, and his own responsibility. The result of the acceptance of deception is that the person will feel alienated."

The first basic formula of radical psychiatry is that:

(a) Oppression + Mystification = Alienation

In my radical psychiatry groups I try to help people become aware of their oppression, to demystify oppression. The act of becoming aware of their oppression makes it possible for these people to get angry about it. This anger is an important first step. Soon they begin to realize that what they thought was a personal problem with which they would have to struggle alone is actually part of a social problem demanding collective action. Feeling more aware of their shared oppression and engaging in less self-blame about their behavior, they are better able to establish contact with one another. This is the important complementary process.

The second basic formula of radical psychiatry is that:

(b) Awareness + Contact = Struggle for liberation

It is the contact in the second formula that counters the alienation in the first formula, and it is the awareness in the second formula that replaces the mystification in the first formula.

When radical psychiatry is successful in my groups, the young veterans leave feeling more a part of the human race and dedicated to struggling to change the society that they realize has oppressed them and dehumanized them so that in the future, no other human beings will be forced to experience immoral wars like the one they experienced.

A radical psychiatrist does not claim to be neutral. Rather the radical psychiatrist explicitly takes sides. Because people who come with psychiatric problems are presumed to be alienated, and because alienation is seen as a result of oppression caused by power-structured relationships, the radical psychiatrist sides with an individual against his oppressor. It appears that oppression can be encountered on at least three levels (Wyckoff, 1971): within one's own head (internalized oppression), within an intimate group, and in society. In a radical psychiatry group much of the emphasis is placed on working on the internalized oppressor. The internalized oppressor can be understood through an expanded version of Berne's (1964) three observable ego states: parent, adult, child. The parent ego state is the one that "knows" without question what is right and wrong. Radical psychiatry divides the parent ego state into two distinct categories, the nurturing parent and the pig parent. The nurturing-parent ego state might say: "Take a vacation," "Go out and play," "Stay away from the cliff." The nurturing-parent ego state helps take care of an individual and to make life fuller and more human. On the other hand, there is the pig-parent ego state. It says: "Don't smile," "Don't touch," "You should be working," "You are ugly," "You are no good." Wyckoff (1971) has pointed out that it often uses words such as must, should, ought, better, best, bad, stupid, ugly, crazy, or sick. The pig parent is debilitating and dehumanizing. It attempts to discredit a person's humanity and keeps a person from taking care of business against the outside oppressor. The radical psychiatrist takes sides against the pig parent.

Two valuable and interrelated techniques developed by Steiner (1971) are used in radical psychiatry groups: permission and protection. Permission comes from a person or people in a group who at the time feel stronger than the person who is oppressed. It is usually the leader. When a radical psychiatrist uses the parent ego state to say to a group member that it is OK to do a certain thing that the pig parent does not permit, then it is said that permission has been given. An alcoholic, for example, might be given permission not to drink. A phobic might be given permission to ride an elevator (to counter a parental injunction against touch). Or a person might be given permission to brag in order to confront the pig-parent statement that says "I am no good." The leader must be strong and sure in what is said and have potency. Permission is always followed by protection. Daring to go against the pig parent is a scary act. To aid an individual to do this, group members provide protection. That is, they offer strokes and support. This is the community of radical psychiatry. It is people who are, at the moment, feeling stronger urging other group members to assume greater strength and at the same time offering the protection and support necessary for such a move. This is the growth and development about which Adelson speaks in the introduction.

Because of the belief that anyone who can help heal souls is a psychiatrist, the radical psychiatry center in Berkeley trains people who want to be psychiatrists. Anyone who will work and is interested can get training. Often people who have become stronger through membership in a radical psychiatry group end up being trained as group leaders. Recently a Radical Psychiatry Center was opened in Berkeley, and the number of people in the radical psychiatry community is quickly spiraling.

Conclusion and Implications

Traditional social science has tended to obscure and mystify social problems. The two major theoretical approaches to the study of youth activism (reductionism and personality and socialization correlates) have been dominated by psychological explanation stressing the intrapsychic and interpersonal. There has been little effort aimed at expanding the analysis to include social factors. Many community psychological services in Berkeley and elsewhere are based on the predominant theories of mental health, which view behavior in a psychological perspective and a social vacuum. Some community psychological services in Berkeley, however, have begun to develop a rich perspective on the psychosocial aspect of behavior and to see the connections between the individual and the society. This is most clearly evident in the Free Church and 'Bridge over Troubled Waters,' which help youth in a personal and social sense, and in the Women's Liberation activities and radical psychiatry groups, which examine problems in a thorough psychosocial context.

The research implications of the psychosocial approach are many. New research questions on activism are possible: What leads people to demand a significant restructuring of their environment to meet their human needs? What are the experiences that lead individuals to critically analyze themselves and their environment, to demystify oppression and constructively change it? How can the idealism of youth be nurtured and retained? How can people learn to overcome the competitiveness we are socialized by and learn to work cooperatively? How can a movement for change relate to the meaning structures (frames of reference, experiences, perspectives) of various groups within the society. These are the questions that will to a large extent determine the future of all men and women.

References

Aptheker, Bettina. Social psychology and the student movement. *The Daily Californian*, 1967, October 24, 14.

Bay, C. Political and apolitical students: Facts in search of theory. *The Journal of Social Issues*, 1967, 23(3), 76-91.

Berkeley Free Church printed a booklet entitled Berkeley Free Church, undated.

Berkeley Runaway Center printed a booklet entitled Berkeley Runaway Center, undated.

Berne, E. *Games People Play*. New York: Grove Press, 1964.

Block, J., Haan, N., and Smith, B. Activism and apathy in contemporary adolescence. In J. F. Adams (Ed.), *Understanding adolescence: Current developments in adolescent psychology.* Boston: Allyn and Bacon, 1968, 198-231.

Block, J., Haan, N., & Smith, B. Socialization correlates of student activism. *Journal of Social Issues*, 1969, 25(4), 143-177.

Bottomore, T. Conservative man. *New York Review of Books*, 1970, 25(6), 20-24.

Browning, F. They shoot hippies don't they? *Ramparts*, 1970, 9(5).

Erikson, E. Reflections on the dissent of contemporary youth. *Daedulus*, Winter, 1970.

Feuer, L. S. *The conflict of generations.* New York: Basic Books, 1969.

Flacks, R. W. The liberated generation: An exploration of the roots of student protest. *Journal of Social Issues*, 1967, 23(3), 52-75.

Free University of Berkeley, *Fall catalog*, 1970.

Friedenberg, E. Z. Current patterns of a generational conflict. *Journal of Social Issues*, 1969, 25(2), 21-38.

Goering, R. 'Bridge' helping troubled addicts. *Daily Californian*, Oct. 29, 1970.

Gould, L. J. Conformity and marginality: The two faces of alienation. *Journal of Social Issues*, 1969. 25(2), 39-64.

Grinder, R. E. Distinctiveness and thrust in the American youth culture. *Journal of Social Issues*, 1969. 25(2), 7-20.

Hall, G. S. *Adolescence.* Vol. 2. New York: Appleton, 1904.

Johnston, R. Aid for addict program. *Daily Californian*, Sept. 30, 1970.

Keniston, K. The sources of student discontent. *Journal of Social Issues*, 1967, 23(3), 108-137.

Keniston, K. Stranded in the present. In S. Garber (Ed.), *Adolescence for adults.* Chicago: Blue Cross Association, 1969. 72-79.

Keniston, K. The other side of the Oedipus complex. *Radical Therapist*, 1970, 1(1). 6-7.

Korchin, S., & Soskin, W. Project community: Therapeutic exploration with adolescents (mimeo).

Mayhew, L. The United States: Changing the balance of power. *Saturday Review*, Aug. 17, 1968.

Mock, K. & Heist, P. *Potential Activists.* Berkeley: Center for Research and Development in Higher Education at the University of California, 1969.

McDonald, D. Youth. *The Center Magazine*, 1970, 3(4), 22-33.

O'Connor, L. Defining reality. In *The small group*, Berkeley: Women's Liberation Basement Press, undated, 2-7.

Parsons, T. Youth in the context of American society. *Daedulus*, 1962, 91, 97-123.

Personal Exploration Groups printed a booklet entitled Orientation to the PEG program, undated.

Potts, L. Progress report of the pregnancy counseling program. Mimeo by Planned Parenthood, Alameda County, Dec. 17, 1969.

Potts, L. When planning fails: Abortion counseling in a Planned Parenthood clinic. A paper presented at the Public Health Social Work Institute on Family Planning, University of California, June, 1969.

Potts, L. Is family planning for the now generation? Part of a panel presentation at the National Conference on Social Welfare, Chicago, June, 1970.

Project Community printed a booklet entitled Project Community, undated.

School of Social Welfare, Community Mental Health Program at the University of California at Berkeley. Preliminary statement of a program proposal in youth involvement, alienation, and drug abuse, Jan. 1970.

Smith, B., Haan, N., & Block, J. Social-psychological aspects of student activism. *Youth and Society*, March, 1970, 261-288.

Stark, E., The Viet war: A women's view. *Security,* published by the Security National Bank, Walnut Creek, Calif.: 1970, 1(5), 1-4.

Steiner, C. radical psychiatry: Principles. Mimeo, 1970a.

Steiner, C. RaP Center training manual. *Radical Therapist,* 1970b, 1(2), 4-5.

Steiner, C. *Games Alcoholics Play.* New York: Grove Press, 1971.

Tannenbaum, A. Introduction (to issue on alienated youth). *Journal of Social Issues,* 1969, 25(2), 1-6.

Trent, J. & Craise, J. Commitment and conformity in the American college. *Journal of Social Issues.* 1967, 23, (3), 34-51.

Watts, W. A., Lynch, S., & Whittaker, D. Alienation and activism in today's college age youth. *Journal of Counseling Psychology,* 1969, 16, (1), 1-7.

Watts, W. & Whittaker, D. Profile of a non-conformist youth culture: A study of the Berkeley non-students. *Sociology of Education,* 1968, 41, (2) 178-200.

Whittaker, D. & Watts, W. A., Personality characteristics of a non-conformist youth subculture: A study of the Berkeley non-students. *Journal of Social Issues,* 1969, 25, (2), 65-90.

Wycoff, H. Radical psychiatry and transactional analysis in women's groups. *The Radical Therapist,* 2, (3), 28-29.

Youth—A View from Berkeley

II. Black Youth

WILLIAM SMITH

The black urban riots of the 1960s generated a change in some aspects of the sociological and psychological profile drawn of blacks in the social sciences. Although primarily interested in identifying the social and pyschological causes of the riots, the social scientists were simultaneously presenting personality paradigms of participating blacks. Not surprisingly, a particular theory of riot causation and its related personality paradigm complemented each other. Furthermore, these newer characterizations of blacks differ greatly from those appearing in the older literature. This paper will focus first on these newer models of black personality, then on the older models, and finally on one possible area of application of the information—the type of community psychological services available to black youth in one particular community: Berkeley, Calif.

Several theories of riot causation have emerged. Using Caplan's (1970) classification scheme as a basis, I have divided these theories according to their focus: demography, differential socialization, blocked opportunity, or internal-external control.

Some researchers have identified the demography of blacks as a causal factor in the riots (Sears & McConahay, 1970; Boesal, 1970). About half the black population in the United States now lives outside the South, mainly in Northern and Western cities. Even within the South a substantial black migration from the farm to the city has taken place. Furthermore, the black population is relatively young, having a median age of 21. This compares to the white median age of 29 (Sears & McConahay, 1970, p. 123). The blacks who have grown to young adulthood in Northern and Western cities have presumably experienced different socialization techniques from their Southern-reared brothers (Murphy & Watson, 1970; Fogelson & Hill, 1968; Aberbach & Walker, 1968; Boesel, 1970).

Sears and McConahay (1970) express ideas typical of those holding the differential-socialization theory. They argue that Southern socialization emphasizes more forcefully the injunction against black expression of antiwhite

Mr. Smith is a graduate student at the University of California, Berkeley.

hostility. They also note that young Northern blacks viewed televised civil-rights activities during the 1950s and early 1960s and were impressed by them. Moreover, they postulated that the geographical compactness of the Northern urban black community facilitated the establishment and maintenance of peer-group loyalties among black youths.

The differential-socialization theory is supported by the fact that younger, Northern-born men played a crucially important part in the riots, especially during the initial states of a particular riot (Tomlinson, 1968, 1970; Lang & Lang, 1968; Sears & McConahay, 1970; Boesel, 1970). Fogelson and Hill (1968), using arrest blotters compiled during the 1967 riots, found that 15 to 24-year-old men were highly overrepresented and that 25- to 34-year-old men were slightly overrepresented in proportion to their respective parts of the population. Even more interesting was their finding that the greatest number of arrests of Northern-born (and thus younger) men came on the first day of a particular riot.

A second theory of riot causation cites the rise of black consciousness, i.e., increased racial and individual self-esteem and the affirmation of black culture and history. Caplan and Paige (1968a & b) found that rioters had a more positive self-concept than did the "counterrioters," those who attempted to quell the riots. As might be expected, there is some evidence that young black people have a more firmly established sense of black consciousness than do their elders (Dizard, 1970; Paige, 1970; and Boesel, 1970).

Another theory is the blocked opportunity proposed by Caplan and Paige (1968b), Gurin et al. (1969), and Lang and Lang (1968). Stated simply, this view asserts that frustrations resulting from societal obstruction of black individual and group efforts precipitated the riots. Sears and McConahay (1970) offer a variation on the blocked-opportunity theory that, at the same, is a corollary of their differential-socialization theory. They suggest that young Northern blacks, because they have a greater set of expectations, are more unable to tolerate the relative lack of progress in the improvement of the situation of blacks in this country. Relative to their expectations, then, young Northern blacks are conceived of as living in a state of deprivation.

The blocked-opportunity hypothesis figures heavily in the theory of Forward and Williams (1970), which maintains that there is a relationship between the individual's perception of internal-external control and his inclination to violence. Forward and Williams cite two hypotheses about this relationship. The first is a blocked-opportunity notion stating that individual blacks have high aspirations and a sense of personal adequacy and competence. They feel that they can obtain their goals and control their destiny, but racism prevents them from achieving their ends. Consequently, they would engage in the instrumental use of violence.

The second possible relationship between the internal-external control dimension and the inclination toward violence is the alienation-powerlessness theory proposed by Ransford (1968). According to this view, the structural isolation of blacks from white American institutions and black feelings of individual and group powerlessness create a sense of despair that generates violence as a hysterical response. According to this latter hypothesis, blacks perceive that control over their lives is external to themselves, while the first hypothesis maintains that blacks believe that they themselves are in control.

Forward and Williams designed a study to test both hypotheses to ascertain the more accurate. Their results were supportive of the blocked-opportunity hypothesis of the relationship of internal-external control and the inclination to violence. They found that riot supporters, in contrast to nonsupporters, felt that they had a greater sense of personal control and tended to blame the deficiencies of the system for the riots.

Crawford and Naditch (1970) see the rioters from the vantage point of the relative-deprivation theory. More specifically, they see deprivation resulting from blocked opportunity generating violent social protest. But for them, it is important that the individual possess not only a sense of internal control, but also that he perceive that the requisite means for exercising that control are at his disposal. They developed a two-by-two conceptual scheme from a cross classification of the variables of internal-external control and the subjective availability of effective means. Each of the four cells is a conceptual representation of a particular state of society with a psychological and behavioral analysis peculiar to each (see Table 1). The first state is found in traditional societies, and the second, according to the authors, is the most unpleasant for the individual and the most dangerous for the society. The term "expressive" is used to convey "non-instrumental." According to the authors "explosive" is perhaps a better word. In the fourth state, the word "reactive" means reformist behaviors aimed at correcting flaws in the existing system and perpetuating the status quo.

TABLE 1. An ends-means sequential stages typology of the psychology of social change.

Ideal-Real Goal Description	Perceived Means of Control	
	External	*Internal*
Low	1. Psychological Stage: Content fatalism Society: Traditional Behavior: Passive	4. PS: Content activism S: Stable B: Reactive
High	2. PS: Discontent fatalism S: Unstable B: Expressive	3. PS: Discontent activism S: Transitional B: Instrumental

From Crawford & Naditch, 1970.

Crawford and Naditch feel that many black Americans, and in particular the rioters, are at the third stage. In this stage, legitimate means for goal attainment will be used when they are perceived to exist within the system. If they are not perceived as existing, extralegal methods will be used.

Boesel's (1970) analysis is probably the most thorough in its recognition of the complexity of the social milieu in which the riots occurred. He views the riots as the consequence of a highly advanced technology and its effects upon American society. In the technological state there is a great need for at least outwardly harmonious relationships between the various sectors of the society. Racism, which had been used by the ruling class as a devisive technique enabling it to perpetuate its domination of workers, was no longer functional. This was especially true because of the entry of blacks into the industrial work force in large numbers. Out of the need to eliminate the more blatant and disruptive forms of racism arose one of the impetuses for middle-class liberalism. Liberalism helped foster an atmosphere in which the civil-rights (and the subsequent black-nationalist) movement could emerge. One of the consequences of these political struggles was the enhancement of black self-esteem.

But at the same time, technology eliminated many jobs formerly held by the unskilled, thus creating the chronic unemployment that strikes young Northern blacks especially hard. They were expressing a greater amount of self-esteem than most other segments of the black community, and they were more inclined toward militant and separatist politics. Demographically they became a large segment of Northern black communities.

Boesel sees the conflicts between the police and young blacks—this presumably also included the riots—not as deviant behavior, but as friction between a newly assertive social group and the defenders of the status quo. This friction is exacerbated by the blacks' conditioned absence of belief in the legitimacy of police authority.

As mentioned above, a profile of the young black militant is emerging out of the investigations of the riots. Caplan (1970) and Forward and Williams (1970), for instance, have presented two of the more comprehensive social-psychological portraits of the militants. When compared with nonmilitants, the militants are described as more antiwhite (Brunswick, 1970), but not extremely so (Tomlinson, 1970). Paige (1970) offers an opposing view, asserting that black militancy is negatively associated with antiwhite feelings.

Militants have more positive feelings of in-group solidarity (Paige, 1970). Consistent with this, they tend to stress collective rather than individual efforts as a strategy for the black community. They attribute to the American social and economic system, rather than to the alleged inadequacies of individual blacks, the responsibility for the oppressive conditions blacks face (Gurin et al., 1969), and for the inability of blacks as a group to advance (Foward & Williams, 1970). There is some disagreement in the literature on the question of militants' sense of personal control. Forward and Williams (1970) maintain that militants do have a sense of personal control, while Gurin et al. (1969) argue that they do not.

Militants are better educated than nonmilitants (Boesel, 1970; Tomlinson, 1970; Forward & Williams, 1970) and tend to come from social and economic sectors of the black community other than the most depressed (Forward & Williams, 1970). They show higher educational achievement than nonmilitants and feel a greater need for achievement (Forward & Williams, 1970).

Since a great number of militants are younger people, it is not surprising that a profile of young blacks, as well as militants, is appearing in the literature. Black youths, when compared with older blacks, have expressed a greater sense of black identity (Brunswick, 1970; Dizard, 1970). They have a greater likelihood of holding antiwhite feelings (Brunswick, 1970; Paige, 1970). They are more likely to espouse radical politics or advocate militant or violent tactics (Brunswick, 1970; Dizard, 1970; Tomlinson, 1968; Sears & McConahay, 1970). They have higher expectations than their elders (Brunswick, 1970; Sears & McConahay, 1970; Boesel, 1970) and are less likely to be impressed by black advances in the field of civil rights (Brunswick, 1970).

The more recent literature seems to present a positive image of black personality. This, however, is not the only type of characterization of black personality appearing in the social-science literature. Gottlieb (1969), like Cohen (1955) earlier, asserts that young blacks have aspirations that are middle class. Gottlieb sees his black subjects, in fact as even more oriented toward middle-class values than his young white ones. The problem for black youth is that they are prevented from attaining their middle-class goals because of deficiencies inherent in lower- and working-class life-styles and values. Specifically, Gottlieb maintains that black parents, particularly the black father, are unable to give effective counsel to their sons and daughters because of their own relative ignorance—relative, that is, to white parents—and lack of sophistication. The father compounds the situation by remaining somewhat distant from his son. Furthermore, Gottlieb theorizes that black youths are unable to delay impulse gratification, and that this inability is incompatible with the discliplined life-style required for upward mobility.

Block (1969) has drawn a rather bleak picture of the black man on the street based on the description offered by Liebow (1967). They are described as having a fractured self-image and a negative individual identity; they lead "fantasied existences." The men are "losers," men who know that society considers them failures and in turn consider themselves failures. Their failure is "confirmed" by the wedding ceremony and the birth of their children. They are portrayed as immeshed inexorably in a vicious, self-perpetuating cycle, which, one may assume, will extend itself to ensnare their sons.

Katz (1969) lists and criticizes the various hypotheses of the causes of poor academic performance by black youngsters. These hypotheses are pertinent because they can, with slight modification, be generalized to explain all black behavior that has traditionally been considered deviant. Katz classifies one set of hypotheses as the "cultural-deprivation" hypotheses. This classification includes, among others, the theories of inadequate socialization, the "mark of oppression," that is, necessarily pathological behavior as the psychological effect of American racism, and the theory of the detrimental effects of father absence.

These conceptions of black personality have in common the fact that they perceive it in terms of social pathology. They assert that a good deal of black behavior is deviant and that it is the product of pathology embedded in black social environments. These conceptions are open to criticism on several counts. Their most obvious error is the gross comparison of black and white behavior and the implicit recognition of white values and behaviors as the standard against which black behavior must be evaluated. Billingsley (1970) notes additionally that social scientists using the social-pathology paradigm tend to misidentify the causes of the social problems blacks face. They ignore the fact that American society is the framework in which black behavior has developed. Instead black "pathological" behavior is conceptualized as a social problem deserving of the remedial efforts of white America.

Third, the social-pathology paradigm militates against the study of black personality and behavior from a black perspective. Questions such as the relationship of blacks to their institutions or the history of these relationships are not investigated. The strengths and resourcefulness of black people are ignored as are black creativity, spirituality, and communal values. Similarly, the effect of these values on behavioral styles is not investigated. One gets the feeling that the social sciences are depicting black life as existentially void and meaningless.

Since he accepts the social-pathology paradigm, Block (1969) can construct a formulation of the abject wretchedness of the black street-corner man. For the same reason, Gottlieb (1969) can make the oversimplified suggestion that black youth want conventional, middle-class lives and nothing more. He can reprove black parents for not being white and for being the victims of a society that did not allow them education or entry into its loftier strata. He can speak of black youth's alleged inability to tolerate delayed gratification as if this trait really had some bearing on the achievement of middle-class status in this society. Gottlieb is unaware that blacks value spontaneity and improvisation in their art and in their daily lives, a characterization that fosters a greater concern for the present in blacks.

Several social scientists have called attention to the pervasiveness of the social-pathology paradigm of black behavior, to the institutional racism of the social sciences, and to the effects of both of these on the racial situation in America. Baratz and Baratz (1970) have pointed out that in promoting the social-pathology paradigm, the social sciences are creating a notion of black sociological inferiority that is supplanting the older, cruder notion of black genetic inferiority. Billingsley (1970) and Herzog (1970) concur. Billingsley stated that the social sciences perpetuate the oppression of blacks and in turn benefit from that oppression. Herzog has called for a reassessment of popular but unproven notions about the causality of social phenomena so that the social sciences may avoid supporting stereotypes.

Billingsley (1970) has suggested some ways of improving the situation. Noting that black social scientists have written some of the best studies on black people, he called for a greater representation of blacks in the social sciences. Furthermore, he called upon blacks in the field to seize the initiative and leadership in the area of black studies. More provisionally, he suggests that the social sciences look to creative black writers for information and perspective on black individuals and institutions.

It is interesting to read the profiles of black militants and the various theories of riot causation. Indeed, my personal observations concur with those of the social scientists reported in this paper. Moreover, it is heartening that the profiles attempt to relate individuals to larger social contexts. This is implicit in the definition of community psychology, of course. Equally obvious is the fact that the newer social focus contrasts sharply with the psychodynamic focus.

Nonetheless, the important practical question is how these formulations will help resolve the social problems that precipitated the riots and these studies. How are these personality formulations related to the process of social change? More fundamentally, perhaps: Who is going to use them and for what purpose?

In connection with these issues, Shellow (1970) makes some interesting points. He notes that too often social scientists use the "step-in, study, pull-out, and report" format for conducting their research. He bemoans the reluctance of social scientists to involve themselves in the social problems they study except from a remote distance and usually in a teaching, consulting, or research capacity. He believes that in order to fulfill the responsibility social scientists have to the public, they should "try to get closer to those in power and engage them actively [p. 207]." He asks: "How else can the social scientist hope to have an impact unless he is close enough to the policy makers to interpret to them his theories, to explain to them his findings and to translate their implications into actions [p. 208]?" For Shellow these beliefs took the behavioral form of his active participation in a police-community relations program and his involvement on the staff of the National Advisory Commission on Civil Disorders.

I cite Shellow here because he does not differ from many of his fellow social scientists on one fundamental issue: he believes his research findings should be used and his services engaged by the policy makers or those in power. But he is aware of one of the dangers in taking this position: "Unfortunately social scientists who have moved close to the seats of power—*and in the process begun to assume some of that power*—have been regarded by many of their colleagues as having compromised the purity of their science [p. 208, italics mine]."

The social scientist's identification with persons in power or his vicarious exercise of that power does compromise him and to some extent force him to represent and identify with the establishment's interests. The social scientist's involvement with big government and big industry is increased all the more because he must depend on these institutions for resources, subsidies, and so forth.

I do not object to Shellow's call for social scientists to get more actively involved in the problems they investigate. And I do not agree that the social sciences are pure or neutral in their relation to social problems. As academic disciplines the social sciences become partisan and non-neutral the moment they are put to practical use. This is my objection to Shellow's advocacy of the social-scientist-in-residence model. He is suggesting that social sciences choose the wrong clients. (Note that Shellow's article is entitled "Social Scientists and Social Action from within the Establishment.")

To return to the profiles of blacks and in general the studies of blacks conducted by the social sciences. Although the social scientists generally claim neutrality and objectivity in their research, it is used to support the establishment. More specifically, the findings are used by the establishment to design social-welfare programs that do not promote basic change but rather tend to solidify the status quo. The cause of social change is not served by the social-scientist-in-residence model. Analogously, the cause of black liberation is not served by presenting to the establishment profiles of black militants.

Frederick Douglas is credited with stating that power never conceded anything without a struggle. Since the struggles with the greatest potential for producing social changes are being carried on daily in hundreds of ways on the grass-roots level, the social scientist should offer his services to persons engaged in these struggles. Welfare rights, community control of institutions, labor struggles, and the establishment of community legal and medical services are just several of the grass-roots struggles social scientists could become involved in. This idea is already being put into practice as young law, medical, and social-science students have begun taking their talents and skills to the community, particularly to poor and black communities.

Community Psychology and Black Youth in Berkeley

One problem takes precedence over all others in reporting on community psychological services geared to black youth in Berkeley: there are very few of them. This being the case, I will briefly discuss a couple of psychological agencies in nearby Oakland and then return to Berkeley and its relative lack of black-youth-oriented community psychological services.

A facility that offers psychological services to black youth is the West Oakland Health Center, which has the distinction of being a comprehensive health-care facility that developed primarily out of the efforts of a community group. It offers a crisis-oriented type of therapy designed to relieve problems. Clients are referred from welfare workers, public-health agencies, and the schools. Many of the youngsters referred from the schools attracted the attention of school authorities for "acting out" or for being "behavior problems." The center uses no therapeutic orientations or techniques geared specifically to the types of problems young black people encounter today. Play therapy is offered to the younger children, and there is some group therapy with adolescents, though these groups are not eminently successful in terms of the members' attendance and commitment to them.

The Family Services Unit is a different sort of agency, handling psychiatric cases exclusively. It tends toward an eclectic approach to therapy as it accommodates clients having crisis-related problems as well as those having more deep-seated problems. About half the clients are self-referred.

This agency seems to be fairly conscious of the pervasiveness and insidiousness of racism. They established a series of frank discussions of racial problems between white and black caseworkers. One product of these discussions was a paper under the authorship of an interracial pair of caseworkers (Fibush & Turnquest, 1970).

About 40% of the Family Service Unit's clientele is black, and a good portion of the black group is middle-class. Although a significant part of the black clientele is young, apparently no programs are designed specifically for them. Perhaps their general approach to black youth is indicated by the type of service offered to a group of black mothers on welfare. The therapeutic goal, which was attained, was the women's enhancement of their initially low self-esteem.

Let us return to Berkeley. John Melton offers a rather unique service to black youth here. He is a one-man anti-drug program. Although affiliated with the Berkeley board of education, he apparently has a great deal of autonomy and latitude in which to implement his program. He performs functions, gives information to elementary and junior high school youngsters about the types of drugs and the effects of drug usage. Second, he counsels young people already using drugs excessively. He defines his goal as seeking to help the person rationally assess his tolerance for drugs and explore his motivation for excessive use of them. Furthermore, he helps the young person understand the relationship between racial oppression and drug usage.

The issue of drug usage in Berkeley promoted the establishment of Totem West, an agency of the city of Berkeley, which was designed to serve black users of hard drugs in Berkeley. Consistent with this aim, it is located in Berkeley's black community. The staff of Totem West is composed of a coordinator and paraprofessionals, and many staff members are former drug users. Unfortunately, the program is not reaching the black drug users but is attracting young white users of hallucinogenic drugs.

The type of psychological "service" many young blacks encounter comes under the auspices of a school system's guidance program for those exhibiting "behavior problems." The young person and the mental-health worker encounter each other under forced conditions, and these are the worst conditions under which the interaction could occur. The mental-health worker is tied to an administrative structure, and consequently, the interaction can not be open and free. The efficacy of the treatment is constrained and its usefulness questionable.

The problem of the usefulness and relevance of community psychological services for black youth is, of course, very important. It could very well be that a community psychological facility offering only a traditional service like counseling may be inadequate for or irrelevant to the needs of black youth. A community organization that serves black youth must be instrumental to their political and social ends, if it wants to maximize its relevance for them.

References

Aberbach, D. & Walker, L. The meaning of black power: A comparison of black and white interpretations of a political slogan. Paper presented at a meeting of the American Political Science Association, Washington, D.C., 1968.

Baratz, S. & Baratz, J. Early childhood intervention: The social science base of institutional racism. *Harvard Educational Review,* 40(1), 1970, 29-50.

Billingsley, A. Black families and white social science. *Journal of Social Issues,* 1970, 26(3), 127-142.

Block, G. H. Alienation—black and white, or The uncommitted revisited. *Journal of Social Issues,* 1969. 25(4), 129-141.

Boesel, D. The liberal society, black youths, and ghetto riots. *Psychiatry,* 1970, 33 265-281.

Brunswick, A. What generation gap? A comparison of some generational differences among blacks and whites. *Social Problems,* 1970, 17(3), 358-370.

Caplan, N. S. The new ghetto man: A review of recent empirical studies. *Journal of Social Issues,* 26, (1), 59-73.,

Caplan, N. S., & Paige, J. M. In O. Kerner et al., *Report of the National Advisory Commission on Civil Disorders.* New York: Bantam Press, pp. 127-137. (a)

Caplan, N. S. & Paige, J. M. A study of ghetto rioters. *Scientific American,* Aug. 1968, 219(2), 15-21. (b)

Cohen, A. *Delinquent Boys.* New York: Free Press of Glencoe, 1955.

Dizard, J. E., Black identity, social class, and black power. *Psychiatry,* 1970, 32(2), 195-207.

Fogelson, R. M., & Hill, R. B. Who riots? In *Supplemental Studies for the National Advisory Commission on Civil Disorders.* Washington, D.C., United States Government Printing Office, 1968.

Fibush, E. & Turnquest, B. A black and white approach to the problem of racism. *Social Casework,* 1970, 51, 459-466.

Forward, J. R., & Williams, J. R. Internal-external control and black militancy. *Journal of Social Issues,* 26(1), 1970, 75-91.

Gottlieb, D. Poor youth: a study in forced alienation. *Journal of Social Issues,* 1969, 25(2), 91-120.

Gurin, P., Gurin, G., Lao, R., & Beattie, B. Internal-external control in the motivational dynamics of Negro youth. *Journal of Social Issues,* 1969, 25(3), 29-52.

Herzog, E. Social stereotypes and social research. *Journal of Social Issues,* 1970, 26(3), 109-122.

Katz, I. A critique of personality approaches to Negro performance with research suggestions. *Journal of Social Issues,* 1969, 25(3), 13-27.

Lang, K., & Lang, G. Racial disturbance as collective protest. *American Behavioral Scientist,* March-April 1968, 11, 11-13.

Liebow, E. *Tally's corner: A study of negro streetcorner men.* Boston: Little, Brown, 1967.

Murphy, R. J. & Watson, J. M. The structure of discontent. In N. E. Cohen (Ed.), The Los Angeles Riots: A Socio-psychological Study. New York: Praeger, 1960.

Paige, J. The changing patterns ot anti-white attitudes among blacks. *Journal of Social Issues,* 1970, 26(4), 69-86.

Ransford, H. E. Isolation, powerlessness, and violence. *American Journal of Sociology,* 1968, 73, 581-591.

Sears, D. O., & McConahay, J. B. Racial socialization, comparison levels, and the Watts riots. *Journal of Social Issues,* 1970, 26(1), 116-127.

Shellow, R. Social scientists and social action from within the establishment. *Journal of Social Issues,* 1970. 26(1), 207-220.

Street, L. Private communication, 1970.

Tomlinson, T. M. The development of a riot ideology among urban Negroes. *American Behavioral Scientist,* March-April 1968, 11, 27-31.

Tomlinson, T. M. Ideological foundations for Negro action. *Journal of Social Issues,* 1970, 26(1), 93-120.

Six Weeks in May:

An Academic Reconstitution Project and Its Significance for the Psychology Curriculum

PHILIP A. COWAN
CAROLYN COWAN

Thurs., April 30: PRESIDENT NIXON ORDERS U.S. ATTACK
ON BASES IN CAMBODIA
Mon., May 4: FOUR KENT STATE STUDENTS KILLED BY OHIO
NATIONAL GUARD
Tues., May 5: GOVERNOR REAGAN CLOSES CALIFORNIA
STATE CAMPUSES
Tues., May 12: SIX BLACK MEN KILLED BY AUGUSTA POLICE
Thurs., May 14: TWO BLACK STUDENTS KILLED BY MISSIS-
SIPPI HIGHWAY PATROL

These events, and the confusion, anger, and helplessness that accompanied them, led to a period of crisis both for those who supported the political establishment and those who opposed it. Weapons were being fired in two directions simultaneously—at the Vietnamese in Southeast Asia and at the students, the young, and the blacks at home. The outpouring of dismay in every quarter of the country clearly indicated that students were not alone in their alienation from society's institutions.

Beginning in May 1970 and extending for six exhilarating and frustrating weeks, the Northern California Communities Project was one of hundreds and hundreds of activities spontaneously generated during this period of great national concern.

"Many students and faculty of the Psychology Department of the University of California at Berkeley have reconstituted course work to address themselves to the extraordinary conditions presently existing in our country. One form of this reconstitution is an effort to bring students and citizens of small Northern California

Philip Cowan is an Associate Professor of Psychology at the University of California, Berkeley. Carolyn Cowan has been a research assistant in several projects at the University of California, Berkeley.

communities together in order to recreate the understanding and tolerance upon which our democracy and our university are based. [Recruiting bulletin for the project] ."

The roots of the project lay much deeper than this specific national crisis. For the past decade university students had been requesting or demanding that their education be "relevant," not only to their personal concerns, but also to society's primary needs—peace, elimination of poverty, and tolerance of diversity in ideology and life-style. The feeling that the university ought to be better meeting society's needs was also being expressed by those citizen taxpayers most unhappy with the present university system, but the lists of personal, educational, and societal priorities of the students and general public were often quite different. The events of last May seemed to crystallize the feeling that the university must be "reconstituted." Many students and faculty could no longer tolerate the classroom-textbook long-range analysis of information for its own sake, while the world appeared to be disintegrating in a hail of bullets.

Unquestionably it was this combination of national concern and educational discontent that led to the creation of a project encouraging students to leave their relatively insulated academic community in order to find ways of bridging the communications chasm between town and gown, young and old, radical, liberal, and conservative.

In a sense it was ironic that the pressure to create a project involving a heavy commitment to fieldwork was so strong within the Psychology Department. Psychology, which has sold itself to the public, to industry, and to the government on the basis of its potential usefulness in dealing with many individual and social problems, would seem to be an ideal discipline for meeting students' desires for relevance. At Berkeley, however, and at most other colleges and universities the curriculum emphasizes a "pure science" approach to knowledge and requires students "to be exposed to" a broad spectrum of "basic" areas of psychology. In 1970 at Berkeley, there were no applied courses taught at the undergraduate level and none in which field experience was an integral part of the content. With the exception of one social-psychology course offering small weekly T-group meetings, the size of sections and classes ranges from large to immense. There are both practical and ideological justifications for this curriculum; the point to be emphasized here is that there is a discrepancy between what the faculty presents, how they present it, and what many students feel they need to learn.

The project minimized this discrepancy for a time, but it was never entirely eliminated. The students wanted to act in order to effect a profound change in the political-social system and the values of individuals within it. Students were not involved in political activity as part of the project in the sense of partisan campaigning for candidates or ballot propositions in the California primaries, which were occurring at that time. The use of the word "political" refers to broad general issues over which legislative and executive arms of government have some power. The faculty shared the general hope for change but saw the field experience more as a means than an end. To them there could be little or no change in values until more was learned about what individuals now believed, about the communities' influence in shaping and maintaining these beliefs, about how barriers to rational communication between people of opposing viewpoints are established and how they can be overcome. It was this fusion of action with an intellectual search for knowledge that justified the agreement that course credit could be obtained for participation in the project if students submitted a paper analyzing their experiences.

The following sections attempt to summarize and document the processes and outcomes of the project, in part to understand the phenomenon itself and in part to consider its implications for the role of community psychology in a regular undergraduate curriculuum.

The Beginnings

To head off the expected large demonstrations in reaction to the political crisis, Governor Ronald Reagan ordered the university and college campuses closed for instruction for four days (May 6 to 9). With all classes canceled, many students and faculty spent the time in almost continuous meetings; ironically, a sense of community developed that had been notably absent on this campus for years. Subgroups were created to consider different kinds of activities. A core of about 30 people (undergraduates, graduate students, and faculty) formed the organizational nucleus of what became the Northern California Communities Project, which was nicknamed in an unconscious parody of military terminology "Operation Silent Majority." (Actually there were two related and overlapping projects—one focused on small communities close to the Bay Area, and one directing their efforts to small towns and cities farther away. We should emphasize again that these projects were only two of hundreds that emerged all over the campus and thousands that occurred across the nation.) While the individuals involved had many different goals, there was a concensus that students would begin to build a base of trust and communication through direct contact with the residents of small California communities and encourage a joint effort toward a massive appeal to end the war.

These goals were to be accomplished by creating teams of 10 to 15 students, with each team focusing on one California community outside the urban center of the Bay Area. There were two major reasons to avoid the areas immediately adjacent to the campus. First, other groups in the university were involved there. Second, urban centers are too large to enable students, in so short a period, to come in contact with the community organization that provides a context for understanding individual views and actions.

The project was explained at two large meetings, and more than 700 students volunteered to participate. During the next five weeks 52 teams each spent many days in communities ranging from unincorporated areas to small towns and a few small cities, as close as 15 minutes from the campus and as far away as a day's drive to the northern border of the state.

Obviously a project of this size needed a large number of individuals to coordinate the teams' activities, to guide them, and support them. The central coordinators (faculty advisers: Ed Sampson and Phil Cowan; primary coordinators: Jeff Martin, Ronna Case, Nadine Payne, Penny Arnoff, Bill Kaye, and Bob Fertman), led by one graduate and one undergraduate student, quickly formed a number of "service units." These units selected the communities, assigned students to teams, acted as liaisons between the team and the project coordinators; compiled, typed, and distributed information packets; briefed team members concerning their legal rights and obligations as visitors to a community; raised money to help with food and travel expenses and to reimburse the Psychology Department for telephone and supply costs; contacted other campuses to encourage similar efforts; provided training in which role playing and discussion were used to prepare teams to enter communities and to evaluate their experiences.

Most of those involved in coordination held the belief that bureaucracy and central organization are the twin evils of present society. Yet, as central organizers and coordinators, they became aware that the project would run more efficiently and effectively with a smoothly meshing interrelationship of the many parts of the "system." The personal pull between values of individual freedom and organizational need led to a number of difficulties. For example, the coordinators conceived the idea of requiring extensive evaluative reports from the teams, not only to gain a clearer picture of the total operation, but also to provide data for future teams who might want to continue where others had left off. Their reluctance to impose orders from the top, however, led to a very ambivalent request for information and a subsequent loss of a great deal of detail for describing and evaluating the activities of the teams..

In such a complex and hastily created organizational structure there were, inevitably, instances in which service units failed to coordinate with each other. They also failed to convey a sense of the entire project to the widely scattered individual teams. Inevitably, too, the organizers, who spent almost no time in the field, began to feel isolated from the project and increasingly uncertain of their roles. This feeling became more intense as the teams returned to relate their experiences to anyone who would listen. For the coordinators, vicarious pride was often mixed with understandable envy.

The Team Members

An hour with any of the 52 teams would effectively serve to shatter the current stereotype of "Berkeley students." They came to the meetings from a wide variety of backgrounds, dressed in the typical college array of straight and hip clothes, and expressed an incredible diversity of viewpoints. During the first half-hour of the first training session, team members were asked to describe what they hoped to accomplish in the community and, implicitly, what they hoped to accomplish for themselves. There were almost as many answers as there were individuals.

The majority was committed to activities that might shorten or end the war within the framework of the traditional democratic process. These students wanted to persuade California residents who supported President Nixon's foreign policy to rethink their position. They also hoped to encourage public democratic dissent (letters, petitions, forums, community organization) by those already in opposition to the war and its escalation.

Many students were frustrated with their image as presented in the mass media. They were frightened by the killing of students at Kent State and Jackson, and they were determined to engage in face-to-face communication in the hope of eliminating or at least altering the public stereotype of all Berkeley students as rock-throwing radicals. Considering the political spectrum of the Berkeley community, it is our impression that very few truly radical students were involved in the project. This may have occurred because the activities were directed toward change within the system, or because there are many fewer radical political thinkers than the image of Berkeley would suggest.

A large proportion of the students felt that they, never having taken any public stand in support of their political and social views, were part of the silent majority. A surprising number were not certain what their views really were. They had dropped out of the traditional democratic process because of their despair at the gap between this country's potential and its present reality. Most of all, the project offered them an opportunity to take an active role in closing this gap.

The Training

Along with the enthusiasm of students to reach out to California communities came uncertainty and fear. The enthusiasm led to a determination to get started before a great deal of planning had occurred. The fear led many of them to welcome an opportunity to meet with one of eleven training units, almost all of which were composed of clinical-psychology faculty and graduate students. In many cases, it was the training sessions that first convinced the students that, while they were in a hurry to get to work, they were unclear about what to do and how to do it.

The first training session

From a statement of goals and a brief description of initial planning, it was evident that the students visualized a number of situations in which they might find themselves in difficulty. They were asked to form pairs and to create these situations through role playing, with each member alternating in the role of a student and a community resident. For about half an hour trainers went from one pair to another, listening and commenting. General issues of content and style were then brought back to the whole group for further discussion.

We encountered some expected reluctance to engage in role playing because of general embarrassment with the technique, and an unexpected ideological protest that role playing runs counter to the value currently placed on authenticity and spontaneity. In spite of the mixed reactions, the choice of roles and the way they were played immediately raised several crucial issues for discussion: how to enter a new community, how to deal with student stereotypes, and how to avoid stereotyping the community residents.

Entering the community. Trainers were concerned with the general problem of how the students could approach a community in a manner that established the team's legitimacy and minimized the possibility that they would be perceived as intruders. It was strongly suggested that this legitimacy would be strengthened if the students were involved in a mutual exchange of opinions and information rather than a coercive propaganda campaign. The trainers spent some time encouraging students to talk in personal terms—not what "we feel" or what "they say" but what "I believe" and why "I am concerned." While the students emotionally favored a grass-roots, people-to-people series of communications, the trainers tended to advocate at least an initial effort at proceeding through existing channels and contacting members of established institutions (mayor, chief of police, superintendent of schools, heads of civic and religious organizations and representatives from the local mass media). It was agreed that proceeding through channels in addition to establishing individual contacts would provide easier and wider access to the community. It would also enable team members to gain information about the community from the point of view of those who influence decisions. At the same time it might help to reduce the understandable suspicion of community leaders who would "hear about" the presence of the team but have no personal contact with the students.

Student stereotypes and the issue of hypocrisy. It was assumed that the students' entry into the community and their reception would be greatly influenced by the way in which they presented themselves, especially how they looked and what they said. After the role-playing phase of the first training sessions, one issue was invariably raised. As the students looked around the room and saw each other through the eyes of the California residents, they became acutely aware that they had to make some decisions about how they would dress when they arrived in the town. Those students who recommended "straight" dress for everyone wanted to avoid encouraging "hippie" stereotypes that would reduce the chance of opening up communication. Some students advanced the counterargument that part of their task was to help overcome society's intolerance of diversity, irrationally focused on externals like clothes. They feared that if all students appeared to be straight, the residents would say, "Well, you're all right, but I still don't trust those radical longhairs you've got down there at Berkeley." (This fear was later found to be accurate.)

Some students flatly claimed that it would be hypocritical if they did not present themselves to the general public as they really were, regardless of the possibility that stereotypes might interfere with their goals. In the same vein they rejected the suggestion of some trainers and team members that they temper the radicalism and rhetoric of their beliefs in order to facilitate dialogue.

The heat generated in these discussions indicated that the groups were not simply dealing with a surface discussion of tactics. For many students dress and rhetoric are not merely externals. Since they form an important aspect of self-image and identity, some students could not calmly consider the question of changing them however important the ultimate goals. Most teams finally left the issue of dress as a matter for personal decision, with some agreement on neatness if not conformity. While straight clothes and hairstyles predominated, most teams went out into the community visibly demonstrating one aspect of the diversity they hoped to discuss.

Sterotyping community residents. A traditional source of friction between the university and the general public is the attitude of some members of the university community that they constitute an intellectual elite who must "carry the word" to a hostile or apathetic uninformed populace. Indignant about the public's misconception of students, team members initially tended to ignore their own negative stereotypes of California citizens. The most frequently suggested role-playing situation was a dialogue between a polite student and a hostile resident of the community. We were struck by the fact that it was always much easier for students to play the role of the resident. Although this was challenged by trainers and some team members at the time, only later interaction with the "real" residents was effective in breaking down the preconceptions upon which this arrogance was based.

Subsequent training sessions

The vast majority of teams returned to take part in additional discussion-training sessions. The number of returning team members, however, tended to decline, either as they became less involved in the project, or as finals and term papers cut into their available time. Some others could not return because they were involved in further activities in the community.

The first training session had focused primarily on raising issues, on information exchange, and on task-oriented anticipation of problems to be solved in the communities. As the teams returned to evaluate their experience, it became evident that some of their reported difficulties in the communities stemmed from the structure and style of communication within the group. (The modal trend in the training sessions seemed to shift from an emphasis on problem solving to an emphasis on group interaction. Many trainers, however, emphasized one rather than the other all the way through. By the end of the project there was still no agreement concerning the optimal balance between the two orientations.) Some of the difficulties and some of the strengths in group function were externally imposed. In a few cases the project organizers had unwittingly assigned two or more clusters of friends to a team, building in cliques and factions from the beginning. Another important factor in group cohesion was the distance that teams traveled from the Bay Area. Those who traveled the farthest usually spent several days or a week at a time in the community. The long drives, the absence of usual social supports, and the absence of other distractions generally created a strongly knit group. Those groups closer to the Bay Area were generally more fragmented unless they made an effort to spend a great deal of time together and establish systematic and regular telephone communication.

One of the first internal issues to confront the group was that of leadership. The team captain or leader had originally been chosen in a hurried and casual manner. He or she sometimes had neither the talent nor the motivation to fill such a complex role. Teams choosing a leader who had grown up in the community were sometimes biased by his views and found it difficult to develop a fresh approach. In a community like Berkeley, which places such a high value on being open and "up front," it is surprising that inadequate leaders were rarely confronted by the team members. They complained to each other in pairs or triads, but direct group discussion of the issue tended to occur only in training sessions. It was difficult to see any consistent pattern of leadership or group decision making that minimized conflict and maximized morale. Authoritarian and democratic groups fared equally well or poorly; what seemed to make the most difference in team effectiveness was the explicitness with which the members agreed to adopt a particular way of working with each other.

Like the project organizers, the teams often experienced a conflict between the needs of the group as a whole and the goals and values of the individuals within it. Initially there was a strong emphasis on forming a consensus that could lead to action. The value placed on unanimity arose in part from the assumption that whatever their differences, the team members were united in their concern about the war and a number of other social issues. The early diverse statements of both ends and means failed to dispel this illusion. Not until later in the project did most trainers view the diversity as an opportunity to examine, in the small group, the same problems the students were concerned with in the communities. In the national climate of polarization it is often difficult to collaborate in solving problems in a way that encompasses a wide range of viewpoints. Students who confronted this issue within their own group began to have more success in dealing with the variety of views represented in the community. It seems that the study of the community, as almost everything else, begins at home.

The Visits

Entering the community

In an admittedly inadequate period of time, students expended a great deal of effort in preparing themselves and the communities for their visits. Many read widely on the economic, social, and political issues underlying the current crisis; despite the amount of time and thought given to "action," we repeatedly heard the comment from students that they had done more reading during the six weeks of the project than they had in the past two years. All teams gathered data concerning the specific charcteristics of their communities and often quizzed one another on the facts about local industry, economic and social issues as they drove to their destinations. Scouting missions, kept small in order to avoid overwhelming the residents, were sent to obtain a more realistic feel for the community than printed material or former residents could provide. The scouts also attempted to arrange for lodging for the teams; some were invited to stay in homes; many were offered church facilities; others arranged to stay at nearby campgrounds.

Preparation of the communities was more difficult, in part because it was not always clear what they were to be prepared for. Before students' arrival in the community some teams sent letters describing the project to editors of the local paper and to church bulletins. There was a concerted attempt to make initial contact with leaders of government, civic, and social organizations, churches and political groups in an attempt to lay the groundwork for further discussion between the team members and townspeople.

Once the entire team arrived, they began to follow up these initial contacts. Many newspaper editors, skeptical at the outset, became quite encouraging in their reactions to the project. Several assigned reporters to the teams and published continuing coverage of their activities. Very supportive newspaper editorials in some towns were clearly responsible for a positive reaction on the part of many community residents and for good turnouts at some community meetings ("Oh, yes, I read such nice things about you in the paper"). Radio stations also provided coverage in the form of news reporting, announcements, and interviews with team members.

In one town the civic leaders were invited to a coffee hour to exchange views on the team's most acceptable and viable future activities. The students were committed to the idea that what they did next should reflect the needs of the residents as well as their own needs. In another town students hand-delivered several thousand packets of information documenting the facts that had led to their personal concern about the war. Those who responded to the attached note urging them to telephone for more information were invited to attend a meeting the following weekend. Many residents, bringing their friends and neighbors along, were delighted that Berkeley students were concerned enough to visit their community and work so hard to organize such a gathering.

Teams had been urged to inform the local police of their presence in the community. Reactions varied from a town where the licensing function of the police was used in an attempt to charge the students a fee for their "daily work," to a northern county sheriff who arranged a meeting of the students and 40 of his deputies. In a letter to the organizers of the project, he stated that it had provided an invaluable opportunity for his men to talk with students in a situation that did not involve confrontation over troublesome issues or behavior. The students reported their own pleasure in discovering the individual humanity and concern of the men on the force.

Types of activities

It is easy to state briefly what the teams did: they planned, they talked, they listened, and they learned. The settings and the size of the group varied widely—PTA meetings, county fairs, high-school classrooms and auditoriums, one-to-one conversations in shopping plazas and on doorsteps, coffee hours in homes, meetings of civic organizations, and meetings to which the entire community was invited. What is difficult to convey is the quality of these activities and the unique variation from one community to another.

Accidents of timing often played a role in the choice of focus for the team's effort. During their first training sessions one team working close to the Bay Area learned that a PTA meeting was being held that night in the only elementary school in their chosen community. Quickly obtaining permission from the PTA president to attend, they were able to become acquainted with some pressing community issues by observing a number of the parent-teacher discussion groups. At the coffee hour following, they were introduced around the room and managed to interest some of the parents in the project. From this casual beginning came invitations to coffee hours in several homes. In turn, the coffee hours led to the setting up of an information table at the local shopping area, jointly manned by residents and students.

Another team found that their community was almost totally involved in preparation for the county fair and did not wish to be distracted with other concerns. From a group discussion at their next training session came the idea of putting up a booth at the fair emphasizing the role of the university and students in the state. To the surprise of the team members, the officials welcomed the idea, and the next week was devoted to planning the booth with some of the residents. Unfortunately, the weather was poor, the fair badly attended, and the booth often ignored; nevertheless, many people came up quietly to applaud the students' actions. Some residents invited students to their homes to continue discussions begun at the fair. While the students felt that the booth itself was not very successful, we believe that the collaboration and communication with community residents during the planning was a positive outcome of the idea. This conclusion can be generalized to the activities of teams in most communities. When residents worked along with the students, regardless of the activity or the extent to which they achieved their goals, the collaborative process itself was an important aspect of a successful outcome.

In many communities the Berkeley students wanted to approach local high schools in an attempt to reach the teen-age population. Knowing that parents and administrators would be apprehensive about the influence university students might have on their youngsters, our project pamphlets and training sessions stressed the fact that contact with high school would have to be done carefully through the appropriate channels. When the principals, and in some cases school superintendents, were given a clear written statement of the teams' plans, many were willing to ask their faculty if they wished the students to visit their classes. The plans that did emerge included school assemblies, debates in history and civics classes, and some discussions with groups of faculty. The topics covered the war, communism, student use of drugs, violence on campuses, and so forth. Team members seemed amazed at the range of points of view of the high-school students. Some of the teen-agers seemed unaware of the impact of the war; others believed it was wrong to question their government's policies, while still others shared the great concern about the war and simply did not know what to do. Attempts to open up discussion with high-school students gave our students a limited insight into the difficult role of a high-school teacher and some better appreciation of the diverse influences in a teen-ager's life—parents, teachers, high-school authorities, peers, college students, news-media impressions. They began to see that it is almost as difficult to reach the younger generation as it is to reach the older.

Perhaps the most frustrating experience for the students were their conversations with individuals in shopping centers and in a door-to-door canvass. Here they encountered the most hostility, perhaps because these situations can be the most intrusive on residents who are occupied with other tasks. There often seemed to be an element of confrontation in any one-to-one conversation between a student and a resident, with each participant becoming a defender of the larger group he "represented." The students became aware that as they were watching the hours slip by they had contacted relatively few individuals on a meaningful level. In terms of their urgent goals, they were dissatisfied. Only in the few instances where students and residents jointly canvassed or manned tables was there any appreciable feeling of success.

From the students' initial contacts grew many invitations to speak at neighborhood coffee hours and meetings of local organizations. The students soon found that lengthy emotional speeches did not have the desired effect. As one stated: "I learned that starting off with an impassioned speech tended to anger many people. It makes me feel better, but that's all it does." The most effective format appeared to be a brief description of the project and why they were there followed by a question-and-answer or discussion period. This allowed the students to respond to the concerns of the residents rather than beginning egocentrically with their own concerns. Several students from the team were usually chosen as spokesmen; although other team members often disagreed with what their representatives were saying, they felt a need to keep silent for the sake of unanimity. By trial and error, the groups usually came to the realization that voicing their varied opinions was more effective, as well as more satisfying. Community residents appreciated and respected this diversity. It counteracted a prevalent belief that "all the Berkeley students are brainwashed by their (radical) professors." (This belief was more widely held than we expected. As a result of activities similar to the ones we are describing on college campuses throughout the state, legislators specifically exempted professors from the general pay raise granted all state employees on July 1, 1970. We believe that this is especially ironic, since in our view it has generally been the students who have radicalized the professors, rather than vice versa.) By the same token, when a resident expressed an opinion he believed to be held by the entire community, he was often contradicted by someone in the room. This graphic and indisputable evidence of the diversity within each group gave both students and residents a better understanding of why solutions to critical problems are so hard to come by.

The largest activity undertaken by the teams in some communities was the sponsorship of a town meeting. These appeared to work very well as long as they were co-sponsored by some local citizens or groups. At the conclusion of one such meeting a man commented: "I don't know why it took you outside people to bring us inside people together, but I thank God it happened." In another town a woman commented: "I came mainly to see how you kids would conduct yourselves. But now I feel so good about the way you acted and listened to us that I feel compelled to consider your views on Southeast Asia and the state of the nation." One newspaper editor outdid himself in introducing students to community members and helped sponsor, arrange, and moderate a town meeting that was attended by 400 people, the largest meeting ever held in the county. Early in the evening one man angrily criticized almost everything that "students these days" stand for. He agreed that the students at the meeting presented their views reasonably, but he could not accept their arguments or, implicitly, their right to advance them. After his comments were applauded, an older man stood up to speak. A graduate of the University of California 50 years ago, he stated that with all his years of experience, he could only wish that he had protested things that he felt were wrong in his younger days. He concluded: "I don't feel my generation is the 'Silent Majority'—I would call it the 'Unconscious Majority.'"

While the applause appeared to be equally divided between those who supported and those who opposed the Viet Nam war, the students were given an almost unanimous standing ovation at the end of the meeting. This was the climax to a week of intensive activity, and after the crowd left, the students sat together quietly on the stage. One of them commented that two weeks ago he had been involved in a rock-throwing demonstration; he felt that this experience provided him with a more realistic and more satisfying alternative.

Each team and each community produced its own variations on the themes we have been describing. The question in the minds of the project organizers, the team members, and the residents was "What did all this activity accomplish?"

The Impact

Pressures of time, methodological complexity and general reluctance to conceive of the project as "research" all prevented a comprehensive and systematic evaluation of the project. Students are increasingly reluctant to accept a role as either subjects or experimenters in social-science research performed in the traditional "white-coat, brass-instrument" model. At times their reluctance borders on an anti-intellectual rejection of systematic methods of gathering and integrating data. Many students, however, are receptive to the kind of action research prevalent in the field of community psychology. In this context the six-week project was a time for students to acquaint themselves with the phenomena and begin to find the important questions to ask. While this is a necessary first step in research, it does not yield the systematic information necessary for a complete evaluation of the project. We were left instead with a series of vivid impressions gathered from students' written reports, from their extensive discussion in training sessions, from letters written by the community residents, and from observations that we made in two communities.

Impact on the communities

Amount of contact. The amount of contact between team members and residents varied widely. In part this reflected a combination of the community's receptivity and the amount of effort put forth by the team. Partially, there was a conscious choice on the part of team members to reach a few people and allow a great deal of interchange, or to try and contact as many as possible with the realization that the interchange would be more limited.

General reception of the teams. Even when heatedly disagreeing with the students' point of view, the community residents were usually friendly, curious, interested, and often flattered that students were visiting and talking with them. While there was an undercurrent of discontent with students and the university (Berkeley in particular), there was also pride in the university, accompanied by a poignant feeling of remoteness from it—a feeling that the students' presence helped to dissipate. Many people responded with great warmth to the students, inviting them to stay in their homes, to eat with them and to meet their friends. A number of residents accepted the students' sincere statement that they were there to listen and to learn as well as to talk; perhaps never before have so many citizens of California become teachers of our students and enjoyed it so much.

Placing the community residents in the role of teachers may have been one of the key events that minimized the traditional negative reaction of a tight-knit community to "outsiders." In a community-focused project the students must have something to offer, but unless they can sincerely convey the message that they also have something to learn, success by any criterion will be impossible to achieve.

Of course, not all the teams received a warm welcome. In two or three communities, vigilante groups warned the students to get out of town; but threatened violence never materialized. Some merchants refused to serve the students and others refused permission to set up tables anywhere near their stores. At some tables and meetings, students were angrily criticized for their presence, for their appearance, and for their ideas. Although they had expected to meet with hostility, they were often hurt, angry, and disappointed when it actually occurred. Those hurt feelings were rarely conveyed to the residents. The students were remarkably "cool" and polite, so much so that other residents often came to their defense, criticizing the rudeness of their friends and beginning to argue with their less reasonable statements.

In a few cases we suspect that the residents' hostility was warranted. One letter that we received described a meeting at which most of the politically active members of the community were present. The students began by saying, in effect, that they were there to awaken the passive Silent Majority. They could not explain their goals clearly and did not present a reasonable justification of the relation between their activities and their university education. The writer of the letter, who was the chairman of the local women's Democratic club, was understandably angry at having been stereotyped in this way. Almost all of the letters that we received, however, were addressed to the project, to the department chairman, and to the chancellor, and were full of praise for the students. This negative letter was addressed to all of the above plus the governor, the local state senator, and the chairman of the board of regents.

Achievements in the community. The students' evaluation of their success in the communities was directly related to their initial goals. While a great deal of antiwar activity was generated by their presence, those students whose primary concern was ending the war felt that the project had been a failure. The political and social structure of the communities and the prevailing ideologies were largely unaffected. (Not surprising in a six-week project.) In several communities the students did facilitate cooperation and coordination among groups who had been working separately on peace issues. In others the students revived the concept of the town meeting and brought people together who ordinarily did not communicate with each other.

Whatever impact of the project on attitudes concerning the war was felt primarily by individual citizens and small groups. Literally thousands of letters were written, petitions signed, and neighborhood meetings held, all of which may not have occurred in such profusion if the students had not provided the impetus. At the time, there were few indications that discussions had changed any opinions (including the students') concerning the government's conduct of the war, but many residents appeared to be rethinking their positions. (A Gallup poll released in January 1971 indicated that the general public over-whelmingly (73%) supports the Hartfield-McGovern Amendment, which provides a specific time limit to military involvement in Southeast Asia—an increase of 20% over September 1970. Of course, many events have influenced this change, but we believe that student activities all over the country played a part.)

Perhaps one of the teams' major accomplishments concerning attitudes toward the war was bolstering the convictions of those already on the side of dissent, people who had found it difficult to maintain their views in the face of majority community sentiment. We talked to one lonely minister engaged in an ideological dispute with his congregation who found the students a source of personal support for continuing to follow his conscience. Other residents, too, found support in the students' presence, their arguments, and their basic faith in this country despite its failure to meet their ideals. Even when students and residents agreed, wrote letters, held meetings, and worked together, there was, however, the let down resulting from the fact that despite all of this activity, the war continued.

Those students who were most concerned with altering the stereotype of students held by residents felt that the project was more successful. In part their success was accomplished simply by their presence and their behavior. It became difficult for residents to hold the belief that students are violent rock throwers when they watched and listened to the students who were visiting their community. The stereotypes were also altered through the process of collaboration, during which the residents and the students found that they had common concerns in addition to their interest in the course of the war. For example, community residents saw the students as representatives of the younger generation, which included their own children. Many times team members were told: "I'm glad I got a chance to talk to you and find out how you see things. I just can't seem to communicate about these issues with my own kids, but now I begin to understand what they are talking about." The residents also appreciated the opportunity to voice their views on many subjects to people who were eager to listen.

Impact on students

By the end of the project we were able to substantiate our initial feeling that the greatest effect of the project would be on the students themselves. Teams returning from the communities seemed to arrive either in a state of extreme euphoria or deep depression. The euphoria came from their unexpectedly friendly welcome, from the intense interpersonal relations established within the group and between group members and community residents, from the feeling of having acted rather than functioned as passive observers, and from what they had learned about America, about what people were like and why they thought the way they did. In view of the students' serious intent, many of them felt somewhat guilty at having enjoyed the experience so much.

Reimmersion in the Berkeley community, however, seemed to produce a case of the "psychological bends." The physical and psychological distance of Berkeley provided a perspective from which to evaluate their experience in the community more objectively. On the positive side, although their initial political hopes were not realized, the students gained some measure of satisfaction from what they had done and what they had learned. They had helped to alter the prevailing negative stereotype of students. In the process they were forced to re-evaluate their own stereotypes of the residents. For most of the students the residents ceased to be a homogeneous "they" and became a much more complex and interesting set of individuals. This was only one example of the way in which the experience led the students to re-examine their own premises and values.

Having initially discounted some of the importance of academic knowledge and research, the students now became intrigued with the questions of how to enter communities, how to think about the social structures influencing individuals, how to understand and alter the channels of communication that can either foster collaboration and interchange or that can further dehumanize and alienate the participants. Some students adopted a new view of what it meant to bring townspeople together. One girl wrote: "For many there is criticism of 'just talk—no action.' But we met alienated people who have been silent so long that the sounds of their voices expressing opinions and asking questions is action! I think it is a huge step."

As we have indicated, the war and the university were not the only issues discussed in the communities. The students saw firsthand the operation of local government and the discrepancies between formal and informal influences on decision-making processes. They found out about many local issues of education, health, and housing. They learned from farmers about the problems of ecology, pesticides, subsidies, and so forth. In short, we believe that many of them broadened the experiential base upon which they were building their hopes and plans for society and for themselves. In the process they began to adopt a more skeptical attitude toward the Berkeley community. For example, one student poignantly recounted her frustrations in attempting to arouse the "apathetic" citizenry of an idyllic mountain town. She finally concluded that she had been presumptuous to impose the worries and concerns accompanying her life-style on people who appeared to have found a peaceful and productive existence. Perhaps it was the kind of intensive involvement surrounding the Berkeley community that would have to change. The next time she returned to the mountain community, she stated, it would be for hiking and fishing with no desire to influence the residents' obviously more satisfying way of life.

Despite the satisfactions and the intensely meaningful opportunities to rethink their values and goals, a majority of the students ended the project in a state of frustration and despair. A very few students concluded dejectedly that only revolution could produce the kind of changes they had in mind, but even revolution was faced by insurmountable odds. Not only were these students impressed with the overwhelming forces arrayed against them, but they were also viewing the consequences of revolution in personal terms. As they developed friendships in the communities, many with people who opposed their political and social views, they realized that a radical and possibly violent change in the social system would hurt the people they had come to know. In many of the final training sessions these students expressed anguish at their conflicts stemming from their new knowledge, their desire for a new society, and their concern for their new friends.

The prospect that revolution could not succeed was a minor factor in the despair of most students who had rejected that idea from the outset. Many of them were coming to grips for the first time with the realities of the political and social structure outside the Berkeley community. They began to understand that "conservatism" was not simply a perverse or uninformed opposition to new ideas. Team members often reported that they had great difficulty in organizing and maintaining convincing arguments for their point of view and that many residents appeared to have equally well-thought-out reasons for an opposing position. Through their experiences they discovered many of the reasons why social structures, by their very nature, are resistant to change. And yet, they could see that their actions were having an effect, however small, and that slow change was possible. This placed the students in an excruciating dilemma. At the same time that they were developing a renewed pessimism about fully attaining their idealistic goals, they realized that only a long-term commitment to personal action held promise that any change in the direction of these goals would occur. Could they make such a commitment, and if so what would they do? As this question began to be raised in group after group the spring quarter ended, and the Northern California Communities project came to an abrupt halt. While a few students continued their contact with the communities and many more fulfilled previous arrangements for meetings, most went home or began their summer jobs. The organizers of the project, elated by the enthusiasm of the past six weeks and not yet dampened by the despair, planned to spend the summer evaluating the events of the spring in order to create an experimental fieldwork course based upon what we had learned. Such were our hopes.

What Now? A Course Proposal. . . .

We began this article by describing the political and educational conditions under which the Northern California Communities Project emerged. By July of 1970 these conditions had drastically altered. Many people were convinced that American involvement in the war would end in the foreseeable future. The university administration, which had been so flexible during the crisis, made it clear that all of the emergency provisions facilitating reconstitution were now repealed. The university board of regents, quiet during May and June, began an investigation to make sure that the campus events of the spring would never happen again.

During that summer and fall it became apparent that the mood of the students at the end of our project was typical of students across the campus and across the nation. They seemed to be putting aside political and societal involvement in favor of getting on with their education as it had previously been defined. It seems to us that this was a time of moratorium in which students (and others) were deciding whether to make a long-term commitment to slow social change, whether to finish their education before resuming their involvement, or whether to drop out of the larger political process and concentrate instead on their personal concerns.

Much of the opposition to campus-based projects like ours and most of the student "apathy" represent reactions to the primary objective of working to end the war. Of necessity, this goal thrust the students into a role, at least part of the time, of political advocates. To the extent that the students were successful or had the potential to be successful, the regents, the administration, and many faculty became concerned that the classroom was wrongfully being used to promote a single political or social point of view. To the extent that they were unsuccessful, the students tended to lapse into despair. Both of these reactions ignored the possibility of immense educational and societal benefits to be gained from creating a regular course based upon several of the project's subgoals.

As the faculty and students gained more experience in the communities, it became apparent that there was a fundamental question that, in the long run, transcended the issue of the war. Increasingly we began to focus on the generic question of how to understand and improve the structure of communication in communities so that people with opposing values can collaborate in creating processes and problem solutions that encompass rather than exclude diverse points of view.

A course or set of courses focusing on this complex question should differ in a number of ways from the project we have described, but it should also differ from the format adopted by most undergraduate courses. In contrast with the project, more attention must be given to academic preparation. The students' final reports indicated that they felt the need for lectures or discussions concerning many basic issues. The course would have to cover such topics as: dimensions of describing the structure and function of a community;

social-system variables affecting communication and decision making; aspects of individual psychology (development, cognition, learning, personality) that affect attitude development and that facilitate or inhibit an individual's participation in open communication; methods of entering communities, gathering information, and systematically evaluating the results. To us these are all central issues in the field of community psychology, but they obviously cut across many subdisciplines of psychology and other social sciences as well (sociology, anthropology, economics, political science, and so forth). Any of these fields, or perhaps a combination of them, could provide an appropriate base for the kind of course we have in mind. In addition to the lectures, training sessions for each team should be instituted as a regular part of the course rather than offered as a service as they were in the project. (We are using the term "training sessions" in a different sense from the sensitivity or T-group meaning. While the groups may touch on personal issues as they affect group functioning, they are intended to be highly task oriented and directed to integrating the various aspects of the course.) Ideally the trainers would be faculty and students familiar with individual and small-group psychology, and also having at least minimal experience in field projects and community psychology. The training groups would provide an opportunity to bridge the gap between theoretical constructs and personal experience and also to use the diversity within the group as a concrete example of the larger issues to be examined in the community.

In contrast with most academic courses there would be a heavy emphasis on field experience as a mode of learning. Also in contrast with most academic courses it would be imperative that the structure of the course fit the content. Rather than a transmission of already discovered ideas from professor to student, the course would have to be set up as a collaborative quest for answers to as yet poorly delineated questions. It would not be realistic to study and facilitate open communication among diverse points of view in the community unless the same kind of communication was possible within the course structure. This process would prevent the course from being used as a vehicle to propagate a single political or social ideology.

There are a number of difficulties connected with the establishment of this kind of course in addition to the practical consideration of finding the resources for staffing it. While we have attempted to distinguish between the political goals of the project and the course focus on forms of communication, regents, administrators, faculty, and the students themselves often confuse the two aims. It should be recognized that no absolute distinctions can really be made. Existing community-psychology courses emphasizing fieldwork in mental-health or educational settings are usually deemed less controversial. There is, however, abundant evidence that such projects also involve some advocacy of values and a particular point of view. In our case, the value we hold most strongly is that it would be good to bring individuals together in a collaborative way. Also, we note a growing tendency to blur distinctions between roles as faculty or students and roles as citizens. Not only on the political left but also on the right, professors and students have been involved as advocates and as consultants to government and civic institutions. Some would argue that this involvement will contribute to the death of universities as we know them. Our conclusion is that pious hopes will not change the trend; therefore we must provide the most thoughtful teaching and supervision possible so that students may use their intellectual skills in a wise and nondogmatic fashion. In our view the issue of communication in communities demands investigation even if (especially if) it should touch upon sensitive political and social issues. As we have indicated, the communities as well as the faculty provide important checks and balances on the few students who would abuse the intent of the course by evangelizing for their own ends. Universities understandably tend to reject endeavors that might produce conflict with communities, but this is not sufficient justification to abandon the idea.

At the present time we believe that one of the greatest difficulties to be faced by this proposal is obtaining approval for such a course. A proposal similar to the one we are describing was rejected in September 1971 by the staff of the Berkeley Psychology Department, although they did approve for the first time the use of a course number for small groups to engage in fieldwork. Some objected that the proposal was "not academic enough" and that it did not contain enough detail. Since the emphasis in the proposal is upon the structure of communication and upon examination of communication patterns in their natural setting, it is difficult to specify the precise content and topics as one can in a more traditional course. To some faculty the large size of the course proposed was a disadvantage, but most seemed to be reacting to what they saw as the political implications. In the current mood it may also be difficult to attract students to participate, but large numbers are not needed to begin it. In a sense the creation of this course represents a community-psychology project in itself.

It is our strong belief that the potential advantages of the course far outweigh the difficulties and risks. The combination of lectures, training sessions, and field experience can provide a context for both personal and intellectual growth. It could serve as a legitimate channel for students to become actively involved in altering not only their own alienation from social institutions but also the alienation felt by many in the communities. In the project we saw a tremendous intellectual impact on students who alternated their time between their home (academic) community and another setting. The efforts to adopt the residents' point of view in order to understand and communicate with them seemed to provide a profound source of disequilibrium, forcing the students to examine and reformulate their own beliefs and values. For us, this is one of the primary goals of any educational endeavor.

On a more general level, this course proposal suggests the desirability of some redirection of effort in clinical psychology, community psychology, and the psychology curriculum as a whole. In the Northern California Communities

Project the training was done by clinical psychologists. Their involvement with a large group of well-functioning individuals and their focus on the community context of individual action added an invaluable perspective to their work with individuals and small groups of patients in distress.

Community psychology, too, may benefit from a new focus. Traditionally (if one can use the term for a relatively new field) community psychology has been concerned with problems of mental health, education, poverty, usually in the core of large urban centers. Almost all of the accounts we have read indicate that efforts to intervene in these areas inevitably became entangled with the political decision-making process and the inability of individuals to establish satisfactory mechanisms for communication and collaboration. It is this problem to which our proposal is addressed.

Finally, this proposal reflects our concern that the psychology curriculum has tended to ignore some important societal problems. This has occurred, in part, because of the lack of knowledge concerning how best to define and investigate them. But we do not believe that a teacher must have all the solutions before he faces his class.

It is clear that psychology is not the only field equipped to explore the relations of individuals to each other and to their social institutions. There are, however, strong psychological implications in these fundamental issues. Despite their complexity, neither the academic psychologists nor society can afford to ignore them.

One of the students summed it up:

> "We no longer see a faceless unity in the Silent Majority. It now wears many faces and has words and life as well as power that we cannot underestimate. We also feel that our team has been beneficial to the town. We made it a little harder to stereotype Berkeley students. We provided the opportunity for them to think and talk about this country's problems with students they could not just fold up along with the newspaper. Maybe the next time one of them reads about the university or antiwar activity, it will not be as easy for them to be as narrow-minded in their criticism, just as we will never be able to be as intolerant in ours. Perhaps none of us will be changed in time, but it is very certain that if we do not come to understand each other, the future of the country is in danger."

Psychologists at the Storm Center

. . . .

The University as an Instrument of Social Action

ROGER W. HEYNS

I do not believe that the university, formally as an institution, should take stands on noneducational matters. By formal official action I mean action through its governing board or executive heads. Because of the ambiguity of what constitutes official action, I would go further and state that the executive head must recognize that what he intends to be private acts are often interpreted as official positions; therefore he must exercise great restraint in his pronouncements and actions. To a lesser extent this is true of other officers and to a still lesser extent, the faculty. But in all of these, the need for restraint is of sufficient degree that people in these categories should at least recognize the import of their acts and utterances. I am here referring particularly to pronouncements and associate myself with the Antioch position quoted in Dr. McConnell's paper: "The only proper institutional stands . . . are on issues scrupulously defined as educational."

I believe the university makes its contribution to social conditions indirectly "by making the results of its scholarship and research freely available" and through the free action of individuals rather than corporately. I believe the university should be nonpartisan.

The purpose of opposing an institutional position on noneducational matters is to free individual advocacy and choice, to avoid orthodoxy that inhibits dissent. The fundamental basis for freedom to learn and to teach has been that the position of individual faculty members and students does not reflect that of the institution as such. It is this independence that is jeopardized in many subtle ways if institutional neutrality is abridged. There is enough evidence on our campus that even an informal consensus on the war has interfered with dissent. It may have influenced the nature of schloarship; certainly attempts have been

---

Dr. Heyns, former Chancellor of the University of California, Berkeley, is a Professor of Psychology and Education at the University of Michigan, Ann Arbor, and President Elect of the American Council on Education.

From a paper given at the WICHE Conference, University of California, Berkeley, July 9, 1968.

made to influence the conduct of the classroom. This interference would be infinitely greater if there had been formal institutional commitment.

To quote Joseph Shoben in "Toward Remedies for Restlessness: Issues in Student Unrest":

> "Academic freedom, it must be recalled, has never applied to institutions; the doctrine of *Lehrfreiheit,* for example, confers no immunities upon the university except one: the right to clothe its faculty members in a special protective armor as they explore *any* trail that may lead to truth and wisdom."

Our best protection, for example, against that most dreaded intervention in university autonomy—the political test of fitness for membership in the student body or faculty—is in the final analysis avoided by carefully avoiding an internal test, which is what formal and informal orthodoxy really represent.

The freedom that a university receives from external intervention from the society that supports it is never absolute; it waxes and wanes, and it is certainly not a divine right. The supporting society, whether public or private, is not required to grant absolute independence to its institutions of education. As educators we should tell them, and we do, that the greatest universities have traditionally been the most free. And we should tell them why this is so: because the untrammeled search for truth and its successful transmission, through learning, is most likely to be achieved with minimum constraints. We can and do tell the public why this in turn is true: because of the nature of the process of discovery and the process of learning. But when we tell them, we appeal to society's wisdom and its maturity and its security. We are not appealing to a bill of rights.

Let me note some established institutional practices that facilitate interaction with the society of tremendous usefulness both to the society and to the university. Although accepted, such practices are not without their risks and are not without their critics inside the university who would attempt to monitor them. I refer to the advisory, consulting relationship. The university in recent years, through its pay practices, leave of absence policies, and appointment policies, has greatly increased the interaction between the university and individual members of the academic community. I believe that most of the federal programs in education, science, health, social welfare, conservation, for example, have been primarily influenced by members of the university community acting as private individuals but with the aid of institutional policies.

Another form of university participation, which is worth mentioning here because it involves university policy and practice, is individual grants and contract research.

I turn now to another form of participation involving university commitment: the establishment of units with a programmatic commitment, the Radiation Laboratories here at Berkeley, the Lincoln Laboratories at M.I.T., Argonne Laboratories at the University of Chicago, the Willow Run laboratories at the University of Michigan. In these cases the university by contractual arrangement undertakes to establish and maintain a research facility. Not all of these have the same relationships to the university or to the sponsor, and these relationships have altered through the years. In general they have been characterized by a certain degree of separation, especially in management and personnel, so that they might be called university-affiliated units. They began with a public need for a particular kind of activity, which in turn requires the kind of personnel and environment that a university has. Again, the needs and requirements of the university have influenced whether the relationship is to be established and, if the decision is affirmative, its nature. Usually these facilities provide research tools that are beyond the capacity of the university to develop.

Sometimes a unit of the university undertakes a study of the effectiveness of a social program. Examination of group health care programs in Canada by the University of Michigan Public Health School, experimentation with fluoridation by the University of Michigan Dentistry School, studies of police in Oakland by the Center for the Study of Law and Society here at Berkeley are examples. Innumerable other illustrations could be cited, almost all of which produce some degree of public clamor when the findings are released. These activities have been defended and protected by the general reputation of the university for objectivity, by a range of such activities covering many areas, by the obvious relationship of these activities to the research function of the university, and, finally but not insignificantly, by the posture of the investigators themselves. They resolutely limited their roles to that of investigators, and even though they had a right as citizens to do otherwise, they did not become political protagonists. The importance of these subtle differences in posture cannot be overestimated.

Since many institutions are beginning to experiment with courses and programs that involve fieldwork (in part as a way of meeting students' criticism of the lack of relevance of the educational experience), since these departures will inevitably involve academic units that have not had experience with this kind of training, and since they will involve universities in further controversy, it is worthwhile to examine what we have learned from our experiences in more established programs involving fieldwork (for example, internships) as part of the training. I remind you that we have had a great deal in medicine, dentistry, public health, social work, education. Here are some of the lessons as I read them:

1. To obtain optimum results, the university must have a great deal of control of the field situation. The students must be geared into the agency in such a way that they are not just considered additional manpower or given routine assignments; real opportunities for learning must be provided. Close supervision by the university is required.

2. By and large we have not found it worthwhile to operate the field agency ourselves. We have in most places abandoned our own schools, for example. We

have greatly increased our use of regular hospitals for medical education as opposed to developing our own. I doubt whether in our new efforts we will ever again establish large general community hospitals; even the ones we do have are different, or ought to be, from general community hospitals under other auspices. Patients must expect to be treated by students, they must expect to be subjects for research, and so on. The hospitals are supposed to take referrals that contribute to education and research in contrast to taking everyone who needs health care. Private-practice use of facilities is absent or limited. Again these are matters of degree, but the emphasis is clear: we are not in the business of operating social agencies. I could go on with this complicated topic, but I want to mention one little-noticed but very real objection to university-oper-ated-and-run social agencies: the autonomy of the community may be compromised. We should be just as sensitive to the ability of the community to determine the kinds of services it wants as we are to protecting our own freedom.

3. The practicum learning experience must be related to on-campus learning. The relation between theory and practice is complicated, and great attention must be given to the complexities. Classroom learning must inform practice and vice versa.

4. The guiding concept for student behavior and experience is that the student is a student—not a general citizen, not another member of the work force, and not an employee.

I think it is important, as I list these considerations, to recognize that there are and ought to be individual differences among institutions. They differ in function, in student body, in the social climate in which they operate, and in countless other ways. A possible service activity might offer great opportunities to one institution and little to another. On the other hand, an institution might develop such a rarified atmosphere with respect to its surroundings that its well-being becomes a matter of supreme indifference to the supporting community.

In summary, I have tried to suggest that while the question of university participation in social affairs has arisen with new force primarily because of the war but also because of the pressure for new pedagogical programs, it is not a new question; universities have some criteria that have served in the past and will continue to serve in the future. There is no question that the university has and will involve itself. Participation always involves risks, and the degree of risk must be evaluated in terms of the gains for the essential functions of a university. Clarity about these essential purposes and clear assessment of the impact on them of any involvement will provide the greatest protection from undesirable interference.

Assessment of Racial Desegregation in the Berkeley Schools

ARTHUR R. JENSEN

Background

In 1967 the Berkeley board of education voted to racially desegregate all of its elementary schools (grades K to 6). Berkeley had only one senior high school (grades 10 to 12), which had always been completely racially integrated. The three junior high schools (grades 7 to 9) had been desegregated in 1964 by making one of the three for ninth grade only and adjusting school boundaries so that the remaining two schools would have similar racial compositions. The methods for desegregating the elementary schools evolved during the first half of 1967. They were approved by the board in January 1968 and were put into effect the following September. The desegregation plan consisted of two-way busing within broad attendance zones that geographically cut across the racial and socioeconomic stratification of the community. The largest school in each zone enrolled all children in grades 4 to 6, while the smaller schools accommodated grades K to 3. Some 3,500 of Berkeley's 9,000 elementary-school children are bused each day. De facto segregation within schools is prevented by the district's explicit and enforced policy that all classes "will be heterogeneous by race, sex, academic performance, and when possible, socioeconomic level."

Plans for Evaluation

In fall 1967, while plans were evolving for desegregating the elementary schools, a number of citizens and groups appeared at the open meetings of the Berkeley board of education to urge that a part of the funds appropriated for accomplishing desegregation be used to conduct a thorough study of the effects of desegregation on the scholastic performance of minority and majority

---

Dr. Jensen is a Professor of Educational Psychology at the University of California, Berkeley.

children during the first few years of the program. The board was urged to consider the merits of an impartial, independently conducted evaluation of the new program. Funds for the program from federal and state agencies were also contingent, in part, upon the schools' having some plans for evaluating the programs that the funds were intended to support.

In pursuing means for setting up an independent evaluation, some members of the board and school officials approached Dr. Roger Heyns, then chancellor of the Berkeley campus of the University of California, to solicit the university's cooperation in formulating and carrying out an evaluation study. Chancellor Heyns formed an Advisory Committee made up of several deans and directors of professional schools and research institutes of the university that had obvious interests in schools and community affairs, such as the Schools of Education, Criminology, and Social Welfare, and the Survey Research Center. The Advisory Committee held a number of meetings in fall 1967 to consider the feasibility of the university's undertaking the large-scale evaluation required by the Berkeley schools, and they conferred with a number of the faculty in relevant departments about the strategy and probable costs and personnel requirements of such a project. I was first called to confer with Chancellor Heyns and the Advisory Committee in November 1967. As a professor of Educational Psychology with a long-standing research interest in the psychological and educational problems of the disadvantaged, I was naturally most interested in seeing the Berkeley schools' desegregation program implemented by research into its workings and effects. At a subsequent meeting, the Advisory Committee decided that I should direct the evaluation study, and in late December 1967 Chancellor Heyns called me to his office to ask me if I would take on the job. I was delighted to do so, although I had misgivings for the short notice, since an essential part of the plan I had suggested was a collection of predesegregation "baseline" data, which meant that the study had to be fully underway in the spring of 1968. The need for this research to get off to a good start by having as thorough an assessment as possible of the schools' educational status before desegregation seemed to me to be of tremendous importance. Here, for the first time since the momentous Supreme Court decision of 1954, methods for studying desegregation almost as one would conduct an experiment in the laboratory could be developed and applied. I had reviewed the literature on desegregation, and at that time no evaluative study had ever been conducted that had even begun to approach what was now possible in Berkeley. White Plains, N. Y., had desegregated its schools the year before, but it was a small community with a much smaller percentage of minority pupils than we had in Berkeley. White Plains' small study of their first year's effects of desegregation had no adequate baseline from predesegregation achievement norms against which to measure changes, and methodologically the study probably could not get by a critical editorial board of any of the top psychological and educational journals. A more thorough effort had gotten underway in Riverside, Calif., the same year, but again it was a smaller community with few minority pupils, and its school integration was neither accomplished by busing nor as complete as was planned for Berkeley. Also, like White Plains, Riverside had not obtained predesegregation baseline data, which seemed to me an indispensable part of the evaluation. In the Berkeley situation, I was convinced, we had all the necessary ingredients for the first major study of the scholastic effects of desegregation. I was determined to take full advantage of this opportunity by designing the most scientifically impeccable study that time and resources would permit by that late date. The study, if properly done, could be a model for other communities on the verge of desegregating their schools, and the information gained from the Berkeley experiment could be of immense value to the nation's schools. The Berkeley schools were pioneering in school desegregation, and there would undoubtedly be valuable lessons to be learned from their experiences. Berkeley is the first city of over 100,000 population to institute complete desegregation and equal proportional representation of all racial and socioeconomic groups in all of its public schools by means of two-way busing. Both majority and minority children are bused from their own neighborhoods to schools that, prior to desegregation, were predominantly either white or black. In 1967, the Berkeley schools enrolled approximately 50% minority children, about 40% of which were black.

An Evaluation Proposal

The Berkeley board of education wanted a contract with the university for doing the evaluation study. Before the contract could be officially drawn up, a definite and explicit research proposal and budget for the first year of operation had to be prepared. This I did in January 1968. My chief aim was to bring whatever expertise I had as a research psychologist and psychometrician to bear on the problems of evaluating the psychological and educational aspects of school desegregation. I had examined previous efforts with a critical eye, and was determined to do a much better job in Berkeley than any I had seen elsewhere, even given the modest financial resources made available by the Berkeley school board.

Certain minimal requirements had to be met if the project was to be of any scientific worth at all, and these I absolutely insisted upon. Adequate baseline data against which future change could be measured did not exist, and to get such data was our first major task. It had to be completed by the end of the spring term of 1968, prior to desegregation the following September. The chief aim of the study was to discover the most significant sources of variance in school performance and pupil behavior. The major sources of variance stem from pupil characteristics (individual differences in measured abilities and attitudes toward school, family-background factors, and past educational history), classroom climate (peer relationship, class size, the particular admixture and interaction among socioeconomic, racial, and ability levels in the classroom), and the characteristics of the various instructional programs instituted by the schools.

Because of the way classes in the Berkeley schools were constituted, random selection of intact classrooms for testing could not have yielded a representative sample of the school population. Furthermore, in anticipation of the longitudinal study over a period of five years or more, it was necessary that we obtain data on as many elementary-school children as possible. The 30% mobility rate in the Berkeley schools meant that all available primary pupils should be tested in order to ensure a sufficient number of chilren who could be followed longitudinally through the first five years of the new program. Therefore, it was decided that the basic assessment procedures be administered to all pupils in grades K through 6.

Outside Testers

The one thing I insisted on above all was the need for outside testers. The validity of the study, I thought, could be regarded as suspect by its critics if the testing were left up to the teachers and other personnel employed by the school district. The essence of an independent evaluation, it seemed to me, was that the basic data be collected by an agency independent of the schools under the most highly standardized conditions feasibly possible. Such conditions cannot be expected to prevail if classroom teachers are called upon to administer tests to their own classes. Consultation with school authorities and with experts in the Educational Testing Service forced me to the conclusion that the only way we could obtain trustworthy data of the kind that a study such as this requires was by having a team of specially trained testers do the entire job of administrating group tests in each classroom. This is essential for the credibility and reproducibility of the data and for having a clear knowledge of the standardized conditions under which they were obtained. Aside from any question of the merits or weaknesses of the tests being used, it is essential that one know precisely the procedures through which performance records were obtained. The reduction in "error variance" and the increase in confidence in the data are fully worth the cost of standardized administration. Another technical reason for controlling the administration of tests is that it permits the investigator to determine the percentage of variance in test scores attributable to differences among testers. We also planned to have approximately half of our testers Negroes and half whites, assigned to predominantly Negro and white schools in the counterbalanced fashion of standard experimental design so that the effects of the race of the testers could be assessed for white, Negro, and Oriental children. We were successful in accomplishing this.

It was to this issue of using testers from outside the school system that the project almost succumbed even before it got started. Some of the school authorities were strangely opposed to it, but their reasons convinced me even more of the necessity of using our own crew of testers. I was not concerned, as were some school officials, with how the Berkeley schools' scores might compare with other California school districts whose testing was done by the teachers, nor did I care if our results were out of line with the previous year's test results obtained from teacher-administered tests. I was most concerned that we in fact should know just how the tests were administered in our study and could therefore do it in the same way in each succeeding year of the evaluation. Since comparisons of test results between different communities, which vary in a host of demographic variables related to scholastic achievement, are patently ridiculous anyway, I had little sympathy with those whose greatest concern seemed to be how Berkeley's average achievement scores would compare with those of neighboring communities. Unfortunately, my hard-nosed insistence on this point did not make me many friends in the school administration. But at a meeting in the chancellor's office of the Advisory Committee attended by a number of the school officials, a board member, and myself, it became absolutely clear that my continuing as director of the project was contingent upon doing the testing as I thought best, and the school officials finally agreed to it. For the purposes of a study such as this, test data obtained in the usual way would not be of much interest to a researcher.

We trained 20 persons, young men and women, half of them white and half of them Negro, to administer the battery of tests to the 9,000 elementary-school children in Berkeley during April and May 1968. All the testers were college graduates, some with MAs and PhDs, several with a teaching background. They were recruited through the university's employment bureau and through various civic organizations in the community, such as the League of Women Voters and the Urban League. Throughout the course of the testing in the schools, a supervisor visited classes to observe each tester in action to help issue a kind of "quality control" of the testing procedures. I personally met with the teachers and staff in the elementary schools to explain the purpose of the study and answer their questions.

The results of the achievement testing especially indicated that the effort to minimize variations in testing procedures by having all tests administered by a staff trained to follow the same procedures was highly worthwhile. Judging from the test results of previous years, it appears that the effects of procedural variations in testing by the teachers tend to cancel out, leaving the overall mean at each grade level and in each school very much the same as when we administered the tests ourselves. But the error component in individual scores is considerably greater when testing procedures are not controlled. This was reflected in the large and significant decrease in standard deviations of achievement-test scores from 1967 and 1968. The decreases in SD are significant well beyond the .01 level and furthermore represent a very substantial decrease in the total test variance, which is presumably a reduction in error variance. For example, in Total Reading Scores (of the Stanford Achievement battery), the variance decreased from 1967 to 1968 by 23% for Grade 1, 28% for Grade 2, and 23% for Grade 3. This degree of reduction in error variance can be a considerable advantage in increasing the precision of the statistical and correlational analysis of these data.

Individual Testing

In order to evaluate the effects of classroom atmosphere on test performance and to estimate the validity of group testing in general, and particularly for minority children, it was decided to administer individually each of the ability and achievement tests in our battery to a random sample of the school population. The children selected for individual testing were not given the same test in a group procedure, and no child was given more than one of the tests individually. A random sample of all K to sixth-grade pupils in the 14 schools was accomplished by taking one child at random from each class at the same time the group test was administered and giving that child individually the same test that was being administered to the whole class. The randomly selected children were tested individually in a private room in the school or in a testing van. It was found that, on the average, children do slightly less well when tested individually than when tested in a group in the classroom, although the average difference amounts to only about 10% to 15% of a standard deviation (equivalent to two IQ points)—slightly more for Orientals and Negroes and slightly less for whites.

General Policies

A general policy was laid down that it should be made clear to all concerned that the data of the project were to be collected only for statistical and research purposes. Any personal information obtained from pupils, teachers, or parents was to be the confidential possession of the project, and teachers and parents were assured that any data obtained in interviews, questionnaires, and classroom observations would strictly preserve the respondents' anonymity. I also insisted that there be no restrictions on the types of data collected or their method of collection, so long as these practices were ethical, completely open to public inspection, scientifically justified, and in no way physically or psychologically harmful to the participants. No tests or other evaluative procedures were conducted without fully informing the superintendent of schools of the nature and purpose of the proposed procedures. It was agreed, however, that information of a personal nature, obtained in interviews, in opinion questionnaires, and in attitude, personality, and adjustment inventories, would never be obtained by the project without the written consent of the superintendent, who reserved the right to veto without question the use of any particular instrument of this type.

Also, in a project of this type, the school authorities should formally consent to a maximum time limit for pupil participation in the evaluation procedures, and all such procedures should be carefully budgeted within this time limit. Researchers need to be assured that they can plan a proper study in terms of available test time and access to classrooms. There must also be reasonable restrictions on the amount of pupils' in-school time that can be used for purposes of research and evaluation. I proposed that the schools agree to the following time budget: (a) the mean testing time per child throughout all grades would never exceed 0.75% of the child's total in-school time per school year, and (b) the maximum amount of time for any single child's participation should never be allowed to exceed 1% of his in-school time per year.

Kinds of Data Obtained

A variety of data were desired for the baseline study, both as a means of describing the Berkeley elementary-school population just prior to desegregation and as a basis for future comparisons. The types of assessment were as follows:

(a) Ability Testing (grades K to 6)

(b) Motivational Assessment (grades 1 to 6)

(c) Scholastic Achievement Testing (grades 1 to 6)

(d) Sociometric Assessment of Peer Relationships with Classrooms (grades 4 to 6)

(e) Teacher Attitude Inventory (all teachers of grades 4 to 6)

(f) Parent Opinion Assessment (questionnaires to parent or guardian of all children in grades K to 6 on a voluntary basis.)*

(g) Assessments of Pupil Behavior and Classroom Climate by Means of Standardized Observational Techniques

(h) Supplementary Background Data

Description of the evaluation instruments used may be obtained by writing the author.

Probably the most innovative aspect of the research design was to make use of sibling data. The most powerful method for statistically controlling for differences in family-background variables is by comparing the scholastic achievements of younger siblings in segregated schools; younger siblings will come up through the grades in integrated schools. Thus comparisons of performance under segregated and integrated classes can be made with considerable precision when we can statistically control most of the variance associated with family-background factors. This can be done most efficiently not by obtaining a

---

*The results of this questionnaire have been published. See Footnote 3.

great amount of detailed personal information about the child's parents or home conditions, but simply by being able to identify all of the child's siblings who are also in school and whose test scores are also a part of the data bank. The more precise and complete this information is, the sharper can be the analysis of the data. Thus even quite small changes in scholastic achievement can be detected as statistically significant, since they are not swamped by the major sources of variance over which the schools themselves have little or no direct control. A number of important questions were posed that the study was designed to answer concerning the progressive and cumulative effects of desegregation on scholastic performance, classroom behavior and morale attitudes of pupils, parents, and teachers, and demographic changes in the community during the first five years of desegregation.

All of the proposed baseline data were collected during spring 1968 before any part of the elementary-school integration plan had been put into effect. Only our staff of 20 dedicated workers will ever really appreciate the effort, patience, ingenuity, and diplomacy it required to obtain this large amount of data on some 9000 children and their teachers and parents in the space of two months. It could not have been possible without the organizational and diplomatic talents of my two tireless chiefs of staff, Dr. Wade Egbert and Mrs. Alice Carter. The scheduling of all this testing in 14 schools under conditions that fluidly change from day to day, requiring frequent last-minute rescheduling, was at least as complicated as playing simultaneous chess on 20 boards, and often much more frustrating. Considering the time pressure we were under, and the tensions apparent in many of the Berkeley schools immediately preceding the drastic changes that were soon to come about, I still marvel at how my staff managed to accomplish all this massive data collection so successfully. These data undoubtedly make up the most complete set of baseline measurements ever undertaken for a study of desegregation. Indeed, they are among the most thorough assessments ever made of a large elementary-school population for any purpose. The analyses of most immediate interest to the school administration were carried out by computer techniques, and summary reports were turned over to the school authorities. All the basic data have remained in possession of the university, have been coded on computer tapes, and are still undergoing statistical analysis directed at answering a variety of research questions. Most of these studies will eventually be published in the appropriate psychological and educational journals.

It is of interest to know something of the climate of public opinion in Berkeley just before the enactment of desegregation. Berkeley is, of course, not a typical American city, and, as one would imagine, only an unusually liberal and progressive community could be expected to take the lead in such an endeavor as the complete racial and socioeconomic desegregation of its public schools. Our parent and teacher opinion questionnaire gives a fair picture of specific attitudes toward desegregation in spring 1968. Completed questionnaires concerning opinions regarding racial integration, busing, and ability grouping were obtained from 337 Berkeley elementary-school teachers (with 71% returns) and from the parents of over 8,000 elementary-school pupils (with 4,596 parents responding).* Analysis of the questionnaire results indicate that: (*a*) the vast majority of Berkeley teachers favored integration and busing and held attitudes favorable to the school administration's official policies in this area; (*b*) older teachers were less favorably disposed toward integration and busing than younger teachers; (*c*) the majority of parents favored integration but were less unanimous in their approval of busing as a means of achieving integrated schools; (*d*) more females than males favored busing; (*e*) there were significant racial differences in opinions on busing, with Negroes most favorable, Orientals least, and whites intermediate; (*f*) a majority of all racial groups favored ability grouping; (*g*) favorable attitudes toward busing decreased with number of years residence in Berkeley; (*h*) homeowners approved of busing less than renters; and (*i*) favorableness toward integration and busing was positively related to parents' educational level.

Obstacles and Difficulties

Since we have no adequate basis for comparison it is practically impossible to know if the various problems we encountered were more or less than would have occurred in any other school system faced with the same invasion of testers, demands of scheduling, and so forth. The time pressure no doubt made it trying for everyone concerned. But there were also problems of a political-ideological nature. For a community of its size, Berkeley has an unusual number of highly vociferous politically active groups that constantly badger the school board and the administration over almost every step they take. This reality, I felt, was often uppermost in the minds of many of the school officials I had to deal with in planning and executing the study. As a consequence, the administration's motives, often governed by public-relations considerations, and mine, governed by considerations of proper research methodology, were at times in conflict. These conflicts were almost always resolved by compromise or persuasion. But I never compromised on any point that I thought might impair the scientific integrity of the study. I was aware that my stubbornness in this regard rubbed some persons the wrong way, but I was more concerned with doing a good study than with being well-liked by everyone concerned. My need to be liked by people in general is perhaps peculiarly low in my hierarchy of personal values. Those who tried to read political-ideological motives into my research proposal, and on these grounds may have felt some suspicion or mistrust of my role in their midst, simply do not know me or my motivations. I

*A complete report of these data has been published: Jensen, A. R. Parent and teacher attitudes toward integration and busing. *Research Resume*. California Advisory Council on Educational Research, 1970, No. 43.

am even somewhat ashamed to admit being such a nonpolitical creature as in fact I am. I have little patience with those who view scientific research as a mere vehicle for propagandizing some particular ideology, and I imagine there may be times when my disdain for this philosophy is not well concealed from the ideologues. For example, I heard it asked, in all seriousness, by one person at a school meeting: "Since we know that research results can be made to show anything we want, why not make them show what we believe in, and what we're trying to work for?" This deplorable philosophy, I fear, has become more common among some highly politicized educators and social scientists in recent years.

There were also the difficulties inherent in dealing with liaison persons who themselves were not in authority and therefore could not deal directly with the various problems that arose. For this reason I usually found it easiest of all to deal with Dr. Neil Sullivan, the superintendent of schools. There was never any doubt of his authority. He clearly ran the show and he had to be admired for the way he took on a tremendously difficult goal in Berkeley and brought it to reality with éclat and aplomb. He seemed to me intelligent and competent, tough and shrewd—traits that I find make a person easy to respect and to work with even when there are disagreements on specific issues. It was clear to me that the picture much of the public had of Sullivan as a mere sentimentalist was all wrong. Such a person, of course, could not have done the difficult job that Sullivan accomplished. I was never in disagreement with him over major objectives, but we differed at times in certain specific aspects of strategy and tactics. Considering some of the thorny problems posed by the whole idea of making an independent evaluation of Sullivan's program, it all went along quite well. Sullivan understandably had his particular concerns as a superintendent, and I had mine as a researcher. It requires some astuteness from both sides to meet the legitimate needs of each, and I never doubted Sullivan's astuteness in this respect.

Politically Motivated Criticisms

Quite late in the course of our data collection, a political activist group, the Community for New Politics (CNP) sent a spokesman to the public board meeting of May 7, 1968 to protest against the evaluation study. A list of criticisms of the study was presented that questioned the relevance of some of the tests, questionnaires, and other information we were obtaining. The accusations and criticisms were so surprisingly false and technically incompetent that one can only suspect that their authors did not expect that any rebuttal would ever be made. A large part of the CNP statement was directed against me personally, alleging racist biases and questioning my impartiality in evaluating the educational effects of school desegregation. All these points I countered head on in my rebuttal at the very next public meeting of the board on May 21, 1968.*

Demise of the Follow-Up Study

My outspoken views, expressed at professional and scientific meetings and in journal articles, to the effect that all of the causes of racial differences in mental abilities and scholastic achievement were not yet scientifically established and that the probable role of genetic factors had not been adequately researched, were publicized quite luridly (once there was even a 2-inch banner headline printed in red) in the local newspapers soon after I became associated with the Berkeley school-evaluation project. This aroused a good deal of opposition toward me in some circles, which, from the standpoint of political and public-relations appearances, undoubtedly made me less than ideal as a director of the project. Many of the school administrative personnel thought I was too controversial to be in this position. I could hardly disagree, considering some of the misleading publicity I had received. Although neither I nor any of my colleagues ever doubted my scientific integrity in the project, it was recognized that the same qualities that I considered a virtue as a researcher, and that made me outspoken in my writings about important educational issues, were also the very qualities that made me so unacceptable to some politically oriented critics. This problem was fully and openly discussed with the school authorities and with the university Advisory Committee. It was decided, with my full approval (although I probably really had no choice in the matter), that beyond the collection and analysis of the baseline data, the project would be nominally headed by the dean of the School of Education as the principal investigator. There were to be two other administrative positions under him—director and program coordinator—assigned to persons not previously identified with this project or even with this field of educational research, thereby preserving a kind of anonymity at the top of the project that is most visible to the media and the public. It was intended that I should recede far into the background, as research psychologist on the project, hidden from the public firing line but remaining in charge of all the psychometric testing and analysis. I, along with several researchers on the U. C. campus in the Departments of Education, Sociology, and Psychology, worked together during the summer of 1968 to prepare an elaborate research proposal intended to describe the project in detail throughout the first five years of the desegregation program. Our hope was to use the proposal to obtain the necessary funding from one of the large federal or private agencies that make grants for educational research. While these possibilities were

---

*Copies of the CNP statement and Jensen's rebuttal are available from the author.

being sought and explored during the ensuing months, the project, which up till then had been funded by the Berkeley school district and the university, came to its sudden demise, just about two weeks after we had begun the spring 1969 testing intended to assess the first year of the new program.

The precise chain of events that led to this sudden (to me) announcement remains rather obscure, at least to me. In the first week of March 1969, the *Harvard Educational Review* (Winter, 1969) published my lengthy article "How Much Can We Boost IQ and Scholastic Achievement?" It was quickly publicized in the popular press, at times with highly misleading distortions, and was especially aired by the newspapers and radio in the Bay Area. Some of the political pressure groups in Berkeley were incensed by these popular accounts of my views and clamored for my being fired, not only from my role in the evaluation project, but even from my position as a professor in the university. A spokesman for one group proposed at an open meeting of the school board that the evaluation study be immediately halted and that all the baseline data we had collected the previous year be destroyed. When the president of the board pointed out that all the data were in possession of the university and that therefore the board had no jurisdiction over them, the board was then urged to dissociate completely from the project. (A few weeks before this eruption, I had been told by Berkeley's present school superintendent, Dr. Richard Foster, that when he first took office, early in 1969, there were people in the community who urged that the first thing he should do as the new superintendent is "get rid of Jensen.") Unfortunately, at the very next public meeting of the board, it announced its decision that the Berkeley schools would dissociate themselves from the university's evaluation project. Our testers, who were already in the schools, were retained to complete the spring testing but all the test results were kept by the school administration for scoring and analysis and the project at the university closed up shop. I was notified of the board's decision the next day by the head of the project, the dean of the School of Education. The same day a school official explained to me that they were reluctantly forced to come to this decision because the schools were not a research institute, but a political unit, and they had to be sensitive to the political climate of the community. This, then, was given as at least part of the reason for the demise of the project. The school administration has carried on with the routine state-mandated testing, but, as far as I know, nothing resembling the thorough and comprehensive research we had planned has been attempted, and I have not found any of the routine reports presented at board meetings very interesting or informative from a research standpoint. Thus a real assessment of the effects of total school desegregation still remains an unaccomplished task for educational research. Perhaps it can be done, somewhere, at some time in the future. It could still be done in Berkeley, because all the predesegregation baseline data are completely intact.

A Personal View of the Issues

From the beginning, I personally favored racial desegregation of schools, and I believe it is coming about throughout the nation. As an educator, I am concerned that it come about in such a way as to be of benefit to the schooling of all children. Achieving racial balance, while viewed by many of us as desirable for moral, ethical, and social reasons, will not solve existing educational problems; it will create new ones, and I am anxious that we provide the means for fully and objectively assessing them and for discovering the means of solving them. I am quite convinced on the basis of massive research evidence that the educational abilities and needs of the majority of white and Negro children are sufficiently different at this present time in our history that both groups—and particularly the more disadvantaged group—can be cheated out of the best education we now know how to provide in our schools if uniformity rather than diversity of instructional approaches becomes the rule. Diversity and desegregation need not be incompatible goals. I think both are necessary. But achieving racial balance and at the same time ignoring individual differences in children's special educational needs could be most destructive to those who are already the most disadvantaged educationally. The allocation of a school's resources for children with special educational problems cannot be influenced by race; it must be governed by individual needs. Making an association, as some persons do, between the "nature-nuture" (or "heredity-environment") question and the issue of racial desegregation of schools is, to me, a most flagrant non sequitur. The pros or cons of school integration have no logical or necessary connection with the question of whether there are or are not racial genetic differences in mental ability, and the outcome of scientific research on this legitimate question should have no bearing, either one way or the other, on the issue of school integration.

Since educators have at least officially assumed that race and social-class differences in scholastic performance are not associated with any genetic differences in growth rates or patterns of mental abilities but are due entirely to discrimination, prejudice, inequality of educational opportunity, and factors in the child's home environment and peer culture, we have collectively given little if any serious thought to whether we would do anything differently if we knew in fact that all educational differences were not due solely to these environmental factors.

There have been and still are obvious environmental inequities and injustices that have disfavored certain minorities, particularly Negroes, Mexican-Americans, and American Indians. Progress has been made and is continuing to be made to improve these conditions. But there is no doubt there is still a long way to go, and the drive toward further progress in this direction should be given top priority in our national effort.

Education is viewed as one of the chief instruments for approaching this goal. Every child should receive the best education that our current knowledge and technology can provide. This should not imply that we advocate the same methods or the same expectations for all children. There are large individual differences in rates of mental development, in patterns of ability, in drives and interests. These differences exist even among children of the same family. The good parent does his best to make the most of each child's strong points and to help him on his weak points but not make these the crux of success or failure. The school must regard each child, and the differences among children, in much the same way as a good parent should.

I believe we need to find out the extent to which individual differences, social-class differences, and race difference in rates of cognitive development and differential patterns of relative strength and weakness in various types of ability are attributable to genetically conditioned biological growth factors. The answer to this question might imply differences in our approach to improving the education of all children, particularly those we call the disadvantaged, for many of whom school is now a frustrating and unrewarding experience.

Individuals should be treated in terms of their individual characteristics and not in terms of their group membership. This is the way of a democratic society, and educationally it is the only procedure that makes any sense. Individual variations within any large socially defined group are always much greater than the average differences between groups. There is overlap between groups in the distributions of all psychological characteristics that we know anything about. But dealing with children as individuals is not the greatest problem. It is in our concern about the fact that when we do so, we have a differentiated educational program, and children of different socially identifiable groups may not be proportionately represented in different programs. This is the "hang-up" of many persons today, and this is where our conceptions of equal opportunity are most likely to go awry and become misconceptions.

Group racial and social-class differences are first of all individual differences, but the causes of the group differences may not be the same as of the individual differences. This is what we must find out, because the prescription of remedies for our educational ills could depend on the answer.

Let me give one quite hypothetical example. We know that among middle-class white children, learning to read by ordinary classroom instruction is related to certain psychological developmental characteristics. Educators call it "readiness." These characteristics of readiness appear at different ages for different kinds of learning, and at any given age there are considerable individual differences among children, even siblings reared within the same family. These developmental differences, in middle-class white children, are largely conditioned by genetic factors. If we try to begin a child too early in reading instruction, he will experience much greater difficulty than if we waited until we saw more signs of readiness. Lacking readiness, he may even become so frustrated as to "turn off" on reading, so that he will then have an emotional block toward reading later on when he should have the optimal readiness. The readiness can then not be fully tapped. The child would have been better off had we postponed reading instruction for six months or a year and occupied him during this time with other interesting activities for which he was ready. Chances are he would be a better reader at, say, 10 or 11 years of age for having started a year later, when he could catch on to reading with relative ease and avoid unnecessary frustration. It is very doubtful in this case that some added "enrichment" to his preschool environment would have made him learn to read much more easily a year earlier. If this is largely a matter of biological maturation, then the time at which a child is taught in terms of his own schedule of development becomes important. If, on the other hand, it is largely a matter of preschool environmental enrichment, then the thing to do is to go to work on the preschool environment so as to make all children equally ready for reading in the first grade. If a child's difficulty is the result of both factors, then a combination of both enrichment and optimal developmental sequencing should be recommended.

There is a danger that some educators' fear of being accused of racial discrimination could become so misguided as to work to the disadvantage of many minority children. Should we deny differential educational treatments to children when such treatment will maximize the benefits they receive from schooling, just because differential treatment might result in disproportionate representation of different racial groups in various programs? I have seen instances where Negro children were denied special educational facilities commonly given to white children with learning difficulties simply because school authorities were reluctant to single out any Negro child, despite his obvious individual needs, to be treated any differently from the majority of youngsters in the school. There was no hesitation about singling out white children who needed special attention. Many Negro children of normal and superior scholastic potential are consigned to classes in which one-fourth to one-third of their classmates have IQs below 75, which is the usual borderline of educational mental retardation. The majority of these educationally retarded children benefit little or not at all from instruction in the normal classroom, but require special attention in smaller classes that permit a high degree of individualized and small-group instruction. Their presence in regular classes creates unusual difficulties for the conscientious teacher and detracts from the optimal educational environment for children of normal ability. Yet there is reluctance to provide special classes for these educationally retarded children if they are Negro or Mexican-American. The classrooms of predominantly minority schools often have 20% to 30% of such children, which handicaps the teacher's efforts on behalf of her other pupils in the normal range of IQ. The more able minority children are thereby disadvantaged in the classroom in ways that are rarely imposed on white children for whom there are more diverse facilities. Differences in rates of mental development and in potentials for various types of learning will not disappear by being ignored. It is up to biologists and psychologists to discover their causes, and it is up to educators to create a diversity of instructional arrangements best suited to the full range of educational differences that we find in our population. Many environmentally caused differences can be minimized or eliminated, given the resources and the will of society. The differences that remain are a challenge for public education. The challenge will be met by making available more ways and means for children to benefit from schooling. This, I am convinced, can come about only through a greater recognition and understanding of the nature of human differences.

Research in this realm, unlike most scientific research, is fraught with difficulties not intrinsic to the research itself. Because I have refused to assume a doctrinaire stance regarding the roles of genetic and environmental factors in the causation of racial differences in intelligence and scholastic performance, I have become persona non grata to the dogmatists at both extremes of this issue. but the personal and professional consequences of my dragging these important questions out from under the rug and suggesting that they be subjected to scientific study are another story.

In a free society, one that permits freedom of speech and of the press both to express and to criticize diverse views, the social responsibility of the scientist, it seems to me, is perfectly clear. It is simply to do his research as competently and carefully as he can, and to report his methods, results, and conclusions as fully and as accurately as possible. The scientist, when speaking as a scientist about his research, should not make it subordinate to his nonscientifically arrived-at personal, social, religious, or political ideologies. We have seen clear examples of what happens when science is corrupted by servitude to political dogma in the bizarre racist theories of the Nazis and in the disastrous Lysenkoism of the Soviet Union under Stalin. Unfortunately, we have been witnessing in the United States similarly ideologically motivated dogmatism concerning the causes of obvious differences in average educational and occupational performance among various subpopulations socially identified as racial groups. Serious consideration of the question of whether the observed racial differences in mental abilities and scholastic performance involve genetic as well as environmental factors has been totally taboo in academic, scientific, and intellectual circles in the United States in recent years. Nevertheless, it remains a persistent question. My belief is that scientists in the appropriate disciplines must finally face the question squarely and not repeatedly sweep it back under the rug. In the long run, the safest and sanest thing we can urge is intensive, no-holds-barred inquiry in the best tradition of science.

There is perhaps an understandable reluctance to come to grips scientifically with the problem of race differences in intelligence—to come to grips with it, that is to say, in the same way that scientists would approach the investigation of any other phenomenon. This reluctance is manifested in a variety of "symptoms" found in most writings and discussions of the psychology of race differences, particularly differences in mental ability. These symptoms include a tendency to remain on the remotest fringes of the subject; to sidestep central questions; to blur the issues and tolerate a degree of vagueness in definitions, concepts, and inferences that would be unseemly in any other realm of scientific discourse. Many writers express an unwarranted degree of skepticism about reasonably well-established quantitative methods and measurements. They deny or belittle already generally accepted facts—accepted, that is, when brought to bear on inferences outside the realm of race differences—and they demand practically impossible criteria of certainty before even seriously proposing or investigating genetic hypotheses. There is often a failure to distinguish clearly between scientifically answerable aspects of the question and the moral, political, and social policy issues; a tendency to beat dead horses and to set up straw men on what is represented, or misrepresented, I should say, as the genetic side of the argument. We see appeals to the notion that the topic is either too unimportant to be worthy of scientific curiosity or too complex, or too difficult, or that answers to key questions are fundamentally "unknowable" in any scientifically acceptable sense. Finally, we often see the complete denial of intelligence and race as realities, or as quantifiable attributes, or as variables capable of being related to one another. In short, there is an ostrich-like dismissal of the subject altogether.

I believe these obstructive tendencies will be increasingly overcome the more widely and openly the subject is researched and discussed among scientists and scholars and the more the general public is made intelligently aware of the issues. As some of the taboos against open discussion of the topic fall away, the issues will become clarified on a rational basis. We will come to know better just what we do and do not yet know about the subject, and we will be in a better position to deal with it objectively and constructively.

We must always distinguish clearly between research on racial differences and racism. Racism usually implies hate or aversion and is aimed at the denial of equal rights and opportunities to persons on the basis of their racial origin. Racism should be attacked directly in the spheres in which it operates by enacting and enforcing laws and arrangements that help to ensure equality of civil and political rights and to guard against discrimination in educational and occupational opportunities on the basis of racial membership.

To fear research on genetic racial differences, or the possible existence of a biological basis for differences in abilities, is, in a sense, to grant the racist's assumption—that if it should be established beyond reasonable doubt that there are genetically conditioned differences in mental abilities among individuals or groups, then we are justified in oppressing or exploiting those who are most limited in genetic endowment. This, of course, does not follow at all. Equality of human rights does not depend upon the proposition that there are no genetically conditioned individual differences or group difference. Equality of rights is a moral axiom: it does not depend upon any set of scientific data.

I have always advocated dealing with persons as individuals, each in terms of his own needs and characteristics, and I am opposed to according to persons on the basis of their race, color, national origin, or social-class background. But I am also opposed to ignoring or refusing to investigate the causes of the well-established differences among racial groups in the distribution of educationally relevant traits, particularly IQ.

Present educational programs are generally failing to provide all segments of our population with the knowledge and skills needed for economic self-sufficiency in our increasingly technological society. Literal equality of educational opportunity falls short of solving this problem. Inappropriate instructional procedures, often based on the notion that all children can learn best in essentially the same way except for easily changed environmental influences, can alienate many children from ever entering upon any path of educational fulfillment.

In our efforts to improve education we should not lose sight of the focal point of our concern—the individual child. And this means the biological as well as the social individual, for man's intelligence and educability are the products of biological evolution as well as of individual experience. I believe that, in the long run, the greatest respect educators can pay the children in our schools is to try to take full account of all the facts of their nature. In my view, more thought and effort should be directed into discovering ways of modifying our educational methods and goals to accord with the full variety and range of children's abilities and proclivities. In that way, perhaps, many more children can truly profit from their years in school.

Berkeley:
A Personal Statement

EDWARD SAMPSON

Writing from London about those days I spent at Berkeley gives me an inflated sense of importance, as though I were preparing my memoirs in exile in the best tradition of true revolutionaries. I am, however, neither that revolutionary nor in exile, but merely a tired psychologist who needed to remove himself from the battleground of American academia if only for a year, lest insanity take over completely. My intuition now argues that persons escape to England less because of its fine tradition of tolerating political deviance, than because England, like a fatigued old man living off his past memories and filled with stern denials about contemporary life and reality, permits one to rest, gather his thoughts, and renew his worn energies in preparation for a return to that still growing but troubled young nation. I sense as well that the battles fought in America are more meaningful and more important to the course of human history than anything one may do battle about over here. So, one can withdraw in relative comfort to rest and contemplate.

But in the U.S. and in Berkeley, as trivial as each encounter may initially seem and as laughable as some events appear with the passage of time and the perspective of distance, I cannot help but feel an overwhelming sense of their broader importance and relevance. There I saw people attempting to emerge from a distortion and compel reality to conform to those ideals upon which the nation was founded.

You asked me to write about my so-called crises at Berkeley (to call up a memory of R. Nixon, perhaps?) and how I viewed myself as a citizen, as a professor, as a psychologist. Like so many people who have been properly trained in the ways of academic life, I spent my early years at Berkeley carefully differentiating between me the person and me the professional. I taught as I had been taught, even though I sensed within myself and within my students a demand for another approach. How absurd I felt when in 1962 on the day of the Cuban missile crisis I was supposed to lecture on some vague topic in social

Dr. Sampson, formerly with the Department of Psychology, University of California, Berkeley, and the Department of Psychology, Brunel University, Uxbridge, England, is a Professor of Psychology at Clark University, Worcester, Massachusetts.

psychology while my head was clearly on the pending moment of truth that might have wiped us all out. So I did not fulfill my traditional obligations as a lecturer, but rather opened up the floor to a discussion of what was clearly relevant to all of us. Was this so.revolutionary an act? From a very personal perspective it was, for I began to realize how vacuous much of the traditional academic material had become and how vitally alive and exciting it was to focus on matters of pressing importance. Soon the barrier between the psychologist-professor and the citizen-person began to break down. I sought not so much to abandon the goal of teaching my field as to find those parts of the field that I could utilize in a more unified manner. This was not an easy task, given the general absence of meaningfulness to be found in most of what passes for "good psychology."

If it is true, as I believe it to be, that revolutionary change must begin with personal change in the minds of men, this small step, probably unnoticed by everyone else, was important to me.

In this glossy remembrance of the past, I next recall 1964 and the beginnings of the Free Speech Movement. Tolman Hall (where psychology is located) lies about as far across the campus from Sproul Plaza as one can get and still call it part of the campus—that is, other than Los Alamos, Livermore, the radiation lab on the "hill," and several other far-flung accessories to the Big U. Living professionally so far from the centers of campus action, I had heard little about the beginnings of that movement until some time after a police car had been trapped by a student sit-in. Perhaps it was more a mothering instinct than anything political, but I felt it important to support those students who were spending the night out in the cold Bay Area weather: bring them hot coffee and doughnuts, I thought. Several colleagues from the department (both students and faculty) and I managed to wheel over a large urn of coffee and serve it, Red Cross style, to the troops on this an early front line of what was to become the campus battle scene. Unlike the Red Cross, presumably an impartial body, I quickly found myself caught up in the movement; for even that night I had to try my hand at crowd control by attempting to keep a group of boozed up athletes and fraternity men from attacking the sit-inners. I called upon all my knowledge as a social psychologist (I did actually review relevant references while the shouting and shoving was going on all around me), seeking first to talk to the leader of the frat group and next to give him a chance to address the throng. Needless to say, I knew about as much about crowd control from my professional training as a nudist knows about the latest Paris fashions. At that instant, however, I cared to know more. While I was in the basement of Sproul Hall urging the police to come in and do something—an action foreign to my later life but proper at that early stage—a priest managed to cool down the situation. Although his success did not convert me to a renewed faith in the religious way, it did teach me how not to handle crowds who were about to clash. It also taught me that I knew, emotionally and deeply, which side I was on. Those persons sitting around that police car managed to trigger in me an intuitive sense of rightness: I knew where my allegiances lay and needed only more time to uncover the rational bases for what I felt.

The years that followed were filled with growing difficulty. With each disastrous course in national policy there came a reaction on the campus that took its local toll as well. It was as though the cost for the national policy some 10,000 miles away was to be paid at home. America, having missed the immediate horrors of war at home during World War II, was at long last to pay the price of warfare. And that price was high; perhaps the lesson to be learned demanded that one finally pay his due.

With each campus reaction, commitments to pure, reasoned psychology were more difficult than ever before. I sought and found support for my own growing alienation from the traditional field and from my presumed role as a traditional academic. In literature I read eagerly about those who at last decided that when their house was on fire they finally had to come down from their lofty studies to help quench the flames. From a few colleagues writing in professional journals, I likewise learned that paralleling the experiences I was having, paralleling the growing revolution of some young Americans, there was a revolution abrewing within the professional field itself.

These literary encounters provided little relief from the uncertainties and anxieties I was experiencing over my efforts to move more forcefully into a nontraditional stance; nor did the subtle pressures from my colleagues initially help me overcome the sense of being a definite minority of one. In all honesty, however, it is to them that I owe whatever release from the bondage of traditionalism I eventually achieved.

The issue of my obtaining tenure at Berkeley flashed a light of insight within me that I think I shall never forget. Like good academicians at a top-flight, high-pressure Big U, I managed to shunt doubts aside while concentrating on my career. I sought mobility within the system by playing the game of research and publication: small, safe studies; small, safe articles. I played the game fairly well, yet apparently managed to leak my real sentiments in obvious flooding abundance. My colleagues must have sensed that I played by the rules while simultaneously deriding those rules. In this, of course, I was at least as hypocritical as many in the field; no proud banner to wave, however.

Whether it was all that leakage, or reactions to my participation in the Free Speech Movement, or maybe just the normal issues involved in academic tenure, or whatever, I was being given a hard time. The feedback I received about the several committees' deliberations "in my case" had a somewhat freeing effect on me. Several anxious months of waiting plus somewhat nasty personal feedback eventually led me to ask that fateful question: Why in hell was I trying so hard to please them? Those who ask this question too early in their careers never make it in the proper institutions. As luck would have it, I asked that question just late enough to be granted tenure. In the process, however, I realized that much of the sham of academia was in drastic need of demystification and that as one of its victims, now successfully passed through the gates, I was ready to take on that role. Armed with nothing more than cynicism and shattered illusions, I was in the process of becoming freed from being a "yes-man" to my field. I knew then who I was and thought well enough of that new-found identity to strike out more boldly than before. Not that I abandoned my professional career; rather, it became more inner motivated and less directed toward being pleasing (leakage aside) to those who would stand in my judgment. I became more important for me to please than my colleagues or my profession. My standards were much higher morally and much more difficult to follow than theirs could ever be.

My next encounter, this time with nonacademic reality, was to take place not at Berkeley but a small college in southern California. In the fall of 1965, I found myself one of the organizers of an anti-Viet Nam protest march, actually, a peaceful candlelight parade through the campus followed by a rally on the football field. We timed our demonstration to occur on a Friday night, while the rest of the nation (on campus) was to hold its protest on Saturday. Unwittingly, our Friday evening scheduling—done primarily to avoid conflict with that college's Saturday football game—coincided perfectly with national TV s demand for protest films, ready and processed, to be used on the early Saturday news—a feat that would be less easily accomplished were they to concentrate solely on Saturday's demonstrations.

I guess that our small demonstration served as the preview for Saturday's coming attractions. That conservative southern California community was flooded with the national TV, local stations, newsmen, et al. I found myself filmed, interviewed, quoted, and generally treated as though I were some combination of a mad scientist bent on the destruction of all that was sacred in America and some famous figure whose every word might be worthy of quotation. Needless to say, those moments of instant American fame—to become a typical experience of many others during those years of protest—left me breathless, more publically committed than before, and more enlightened about the so-called dynamics of protest demonstrations. I found myself the victim, as it were, of letters from angry citizens; I was the incarnation of evil for many of the local newspapers, one of which referred to me as an outside Communist agitator sent down from Berkeley to stir up trouble; and last, but not least, I became the target of my colleagues' angry and barely intellectual barbs. Small was descriptive of more than that college.

On return to Berkeley, I found it easy to slip again into that community's spirit. Causes were rampant, inspired by events off the campus and typical administrative overreaction on the campus. The summer of 1968 found the Berkeley community itself in open street battle with the local police after what was ostensibly a celebration in support of the French students' revolt became in reality a local replay. During that period, I experienced my first taste of street battling and urban warfare American style. (Actually my second, since in 1967 I had experienced the hippie scene in the Haight-Ashbury district of San Francisco under the ever watchful eye and ready baton of the S.F. police department.)

Along with many others, I was tear gassed repeatedly, chased more often than I can now recall. I, the professor, found myself diving headlong into bushes to avoid detection by police patrols and jumping over fences to hide in strange basements while the police attacked those less fortunate. I usually experienced enough distance from these personal happenings to sense a certain ridiculous quality about the entire matter: "U.C. prof and several students cringe in bushes on campus while tear gas falls down around them and police jab their clubs about in search of the escaped agitators." More often than not, I felt that I was a character in some old Hollywood spy thriller. Dutifully, like my co-conspirators and our type-cast enemy, the police, I played out my role; and none of us in either part needed any direction to know where to turn and how to act. Soon, these routines became almost second nature. One could foretell when the gas would come, when the clubs would be swung, when running was required, or when a suit and tie would serve as a Superman's shield against the still discriminating police avengers.

It was in the middle of that summer that I found myself a participant in what was to become for me a key event, one that became central to the life of the Berkeley campus itself. Approached by a student and friend, I was asked if I would be willing to help sponsor a student-initiated course on racism in which Eldridge Cleaver would be a major lecturer. The idea sounded great to me, so I agreed. Little did I know at that moment just how that facile agreement would plunge me into a sequence of events that not only thrust me once again before the public—earning me the usual batch of reflexive hate mail declaring me a Commie-Jew-homosexual-nigger-loving-bastard—but also cast me and my colleagues in this endeavor in the role of hero to some and definite enemy material to others. The latter were by far in the majority. The issue, on its face so simple, to permit a noted black militant author a platform in a classroom where his views could both be expressed and critically examined, at once became complicated by the intervention of Governor Ronald Reagan and his Board of Regents. They used every avenue open to them to deny facilities on the campus and academic credit to the Cleaver course, forcing us to stand up in defiance over what we saw as inappropriate outside interference in a legitimate faculty matter. It was during that time that my fellow sponsors and I were locked up day after day in meeting after meeting far into the night seeking to match our moves to the anticipated moves of the university powers. Quite a game it was too. We had no room on campus for our class to begin, and here it was only a week away from its opening day. The chancellor, following regental directives, refused us facilities for the course; we sought means of negotiation, going so far on one Sunday evening about 9 to meet with the chancellor and his key assistant to discuss the entire matter. I remember his words quite vividly, mainly because I kept a diary of the affair: he said that it would be definitely *therapeutic* for the entire university if we just dropped the Cleaver course. He did not want to order us into this kind of therapy; he only wished us to consider the political realities in California, as though these had escaped us over the weeks preceding that meeting. We saw our role as defending the principle of academic freedom against the threats posed by the governor and the often ill-informed public he purported to represent.

If we gave in now, the entire concept of academic freedom would be distorted in the name of Reagan's particularly distorted view of education. If we did not give in, however, we had no room on campus in which to meet and hold the class; to complicate it further, our more militant associates threatened to take a room by force. We stuck it out. Two days or so before the class was to begin, we finally obtained a room. The chancellor saw a way thru the regental muck; this was not to be considered a class, only a program of study, not held for credit; thus it could be given a university room just as a string quartet might be. We felt it to be a regular course, fully deserving credit, but did not wish to argue that point at that particular moment. After all, we had got our room and the class would begin.

The moment of Cleaver's entrance arrived. The press clogged the outside of the lecture hall; we had posted our own guards at the doors, letting in only authorized students, i.e., those who had officially registered with us for the course. A few unofficial persons slipped by as well. Jerry Rubin got in while one of the regents' aides was denied entry (they had no passes!). Naturally, this caused a great outcry of foul play. (Fascinating how at first they say "no Cleaver," and then when he is to arrive they want to see him, and cry out when what they forbid is not handled as they wish!) On that day, the total scene was more like a circus than a classroom. Cleaver made his entrance and began the first of his series of lectures. Many students were disappointed; they expected at least a few shouts of motherfucker; rather, they heard a more or less academic analysis of the meaning of being black.

As one might expect, the excitement died down with the passage of time; the throngs of the first session dwindled as did the once eager but now sated Berkeley press corps. But we kept on with the course. True to their role as catalysts to militant causes, the regents passed new proclamations to ensure that the course would never receive credit in any form whatsoever. And true to their cause, a group of dedicated students in the course sought peacefully to petition the administration by a Sproul Hall sit-in. And true to its role, the administration felt compelled to call out the police, who true to their role arrested all in sight, even me. But I was rapidly released on the word of the dean of students, who said that I was inside this locked building as a calming agent. (It is funny how a sit-in runs. Everyone is told to leave and then the building is locked. Inside, however, in addition to the students—carefully labeled as those who are trespassing in violation of the law—one finds about 50 newsmen and TV camera crews, assorted faculty observers, several deans and assistant deans, people from the chancellor's office, and of course, the police. Quite a crowd for a locked building. Puzzling to me is that if this one group there is trespassing, why all those others are not.)

When we were all locked in the building, and the statement had been made that arrests were likely, I kept asking myself just who I was. Was I the professor meeting with his students? Was I the social psychologist taking this firsthand opportunity to study a sit-in, as some of my colleagues had done during the FSM days? Or was I in reality sitting in with my students to protest the policing of the regents as enforced by the administration? I never got a chance to answer that question, for just as I was mulling it over once again—about the 100th time that evening—the police came, and much to my surprise took me off. But I was one of the lucky ones, released even before any official arrest had been declared. With my blood now boiling with excitement and anger, I could not easily think then of a calm return to the classroom with its business as usual.

Well, I could go on to relate more about the Cleaver affair, how we spent endless days in additional meetings, how I sought to give students credit through independent study, how that was eventually denied, how we finally sought redress in the courts, and on, and on. I could go on to relate the events that occurred around the Third World strike and the People's Park episodes, how during the latter some colleagues and I sought to maintain a faculty vigil in defiance of the governor's emergency orders banning any public gatherings; how we not only maintained the vigil but kept up daily marches around the campus and to the community, seeking to break through the National Guard lines before they could re-form and trap us once again on the campus, once again easy targets for their gassings, clubbings, shootings. I could go on to relate the events that occurred on campus after the Cambodian invasion, when we reconstituted our classes, sending students into the community to apply the principles of social psychology or to study them in a natural context, only to be rebuffed in these efforts by a narrow conception of "proper education."

The events blur in my mind. Let me try to step outside that blur, painful even now as I try to remember the moments of excitement, the moments in which there was a real feeling of joint accomplishment, and those more numerous moments of gloom and defeat when all seemed so ponderously unchangeable, in spite of all that one might do. Let me return to me the citizen and me the professional.

My roles blur and cross as I think they must inevitably, at least for me. I can no longer easily dwell in comfort as a professor for eight hours or so each day and in outrage as a citizen for the remainder of the time. My life, as lived, is a unity, not neatly differentiated into my profession and my values. Perhaps I live in an idealistic dream world. I cannot easily teach abstractly without personal relevance and reference to what I have experienced and know too deeply to doubt its reality. There are some experiences and some events that have had too profound an impact on me to be denied as I practice my profession. I can no longer face a group of students, of whatever persuasion, and feed them what passes for the accumulated wisdom of psychology, without commenting; or direct them to methods of investigation that seek to be manipulative and destructive of human dignity and welfare. I cannot easily stand idly by as though there was nothing going on and present the time-honored tradition of a field that went astray and needs desperately to find itself while it is still worthwhile and there is still time. I can neither ignore the anxieties I see in my students' faces nor deny the feelings they freely tell me, as though in the name of so-called social science, their lives and experiences are irrelevant.

Yet the intellectually curious professional, which is so deeply ingrained within me that it is as much a part of my makeup as is my apparent passion for dissent, calls upon me to use my experiences and others' as a continuing source of psychological data. I find myself, in fact, a most interesting subject to study and to learn about. One cannot long run about on picket lines, join in demonstrations, witness violence on the campus and in the streets, without wondering why. I am participant and observer, jumping from one perspective to the other, and feeling all the while that this is both a legitimate form of investigation and one that may be important for the modern psychologist who wishes to understand human life and behavior, including his own.

There are times, however, in which I wish, almost desperately, that I had no doubts any more about my mixed system of roles and my blurred commitments as both a citizen and a professional. There are times I wish I was more of a participant and less of an observer. I wish for less doubt, I think, so that I could be truly revolutionary and not just a half-hearted one. But I think too much, act not reflexively enough, and ponder motivations too deeply to participate in the manner that others are.

I wish for less doubt, I think, so that I could perhaps again be a more traditional psychologist and earn the honors my field hands out to its proper citizens. I exist as a marginal man between two worlds, really not a part of either, yet at moments longing for full membership in one or the other.

Would that I could run another experiment in the manner I once did and not question my motives so much or ponder over the often meaningless quality this kind of game has.

Would that I could join a band of true revolutionaries and plan and enact the visions that so many talk about, without questioning too much and too deeply the meaning of these actions as well.

Though caught upon the horns of my marginality, a position that should lead to inaction, I cannot remain standing by idly either; for me, knowledge implies action, and out of action comes knowledge. The two are so intimately linked that one (this one, at least) cannot wait for a personal dilemma to be resolved; rather, I see myself as moving as far in a given direction as I can go without upsetting the pull from the other side. (See, there I go thinking and analyzing again.) At times, this means that I abandon all hopes of ever returning to the psychological fold as I strike out in protest; yet, as though cursed forever, just as I feel those impulses driving me to take that major step into revolutionary activity, my mind moves in with analyses, questions, values, and genuine intellectual curiosity: this holds me in check. I take little solace that others are in this same boat today or that others have likewise been throughout history. Each man's reliving of history is, whatever else, his own history.

One day, my doubt may pass and I may find myself no longer slipping into the observer's professional role, no longer critically questioning the dynamics of my own actions and those of my colleagues in these change-oriented endeavors. When and if that day arrives, I will undoubtedly no longer be asked to write as I am now doing, and I will undoubtedly no longer wish to write. For I would then find writing a tedium, an occupier of time that is better spent elsewhere; I would find telling others a tedium, wasted effort when more coercive tactics are necessary. But I have not yet reached that point, so I still write, I still talk, I still doubt, and I still wonder.

Perhaps there is room for a variety of commitments both as a citizen and as a professional. But I am uneasy with mine. I am still persuaded intellectually by the arguments of those among my colleagues who told me often and in various ways to "cool it," who maintained that one cannot let his values intervene in that manner in his professional life. Yet at just that moment when I feel myself backsliding, I need only turn on the TV, or pick up a newspaper, or face a classroom of students to know that once again the battle is on. I lose patience then with those who dawdle when time has passed us by. I lose patience with those who want to go slowly when I sense that unless there are some who call for revolution, "go slowly" will rule the day. I grow impatient more and more of the time. With that impatience, my doubt vanishes and I am once again ready to fight within the belly of the monster.

So you see I have not resolved the real dilemma facing the person who would be an academic and an actively concerned citizen. Even as I most sourly criticize my colleagues for their lack of commitment, I am caught up wrestling with my own. Even as I denounce the extremes of violent protest, I hear an almost too-understanding voice within me nod an intuitive assent.

The professional who would face the community, of course, may never come to grips with these kinds of personal issues. One can participate in more benign (i.e., less revolutionary) programs of community work that, though inevitably caught up with politics and values, may offer a lesser conflict over the citizen-professional dilemma. But for those who would participate in more radical forms of change, these more extreme dilemmas are fundamental. In spite of the uncertainties and anxieties that can result, I think that it is increasingly urgent that the psychological community dare to tread the paths of social change. Of this, at least, I have little doubt: change is taking place and will continue to take place, whether or not psychologists intervene. Those professionals who as citizens wish to have something to say about the nature of these changes owe it to themselves at minimum, and surely to their profession, to become involved. It is only a philosopher, and not a good one at that, who would not soil his hands in helping another person if he saw him heading rapidly down a road and knew (or thought he did) that the bridge had been recently washed away.

I am not certain if this is the kind of statement you wanted, or if this is really the best statement that I could give. From my rest haven here in England, I find that writing about my life at Berkeley brings on feelings that I am trying to store away for this year of hoped-for rest. There is a deep sense of guilt within me for having left my friends and colleagues behind while I have wandered off in search of a moment's peace. Writing this brings those feelings into the kind of salience that is almost too disruptive.

I do not think that I was born to rest, as much as I might wish it to be so; there is within me a certain something that demands expression, even now and even here in England. I am not sure who will be reading this, what they will be looking for, or even why. But for those who are trying to find answers here, I have none. For those who are looking for references to cite, I offer none. For those who are seeking a psychologist's intellectual analysis of his position in protest, I offer little other than this psychologist's brief encounters, briefly noted. Most of the people I know will not need to read this, for their own stories as lived are better than mine as written. What can be better, I wonder, than to live one's own story of which one is the author? Much better, in fact, than living another's.

Points and Counterpoints

. . . .

In these papers are reflected the different values of our larger society and of these individual psychologists. Whether as citizens or as scientists, psychologists also are committed implicitly or explicitly to certain positions with respect to community and social problems which form a base for their areas of investigation, their hypotheses, their instruments and methodologies, and their interpretations of findings.

One focus of community psychology may be seen as "man's encounter with history;" whether we are concerned with the definition of community as shared or common destiny of ethnic, national, professional, self-help, youth or other groups or with a definition of community as a system of systems—such as family, school, industry, university, psychology class—each with its own history.

In Berkeley, Heynes, Jensen, and Sampson stood in an encounter with history—each from a different vantage point which shaped this perspective and actions. Each also carried a set of values or commitments which would shape his actions no matter what the vantage point: Heynes concerned with keeping the University a place of free inquiry; Jensen with doing a "scientific" evaluation using established instruments and methodologies; and Sampson with questions around the relevance of psychology for social problems.

The reader may assess for himself how he sees these men. In this assessment he shall also be defining something about himself, and he may even have some insight as to where he stands as citizen and psychologist through this revelation.

D. A.